RECLAMATION

RECLAMATION

Breaking the Chains of Racism and Police Brutality

Vashti Sherrod

TYMM PUBLISHING
COLUMBIA, SC

Reclamation
Breaking the Chains of Racism and Police Brutality

This book is a work of non-fiction based on the life, experiences, and recollections of the author. All but names and some locations have been changed to protect their privacy. The author has indicated the contents of this book are true.

Paperback ISBN: 978-1-7363631-0-2
Ebook ISBN: 978-1-7363631-1-9

Publishing Assistance: Tymm Publishing LLC
Copy Editing: Felicia Murrell
Cover and Book Design: Tywebbin Creations LLC

CONTENTS

PART TWO

DEDICATION

To my daughter Ginger DeMille whose support from the beginning of our traumatic journey and unwavering devotion, inspiration, and encouragement helped me to achieve writing this book. When PTSD and writer's block set in, Ginger displayed her talent as an accomplished pianist by playing Beethoven's "Moonlight Sonata," which unblocked the block. She is my angel!

ACKNOWLEDGEMENTS

First, thank you to my husband, Eugene Sherrod for his love and support through this traumatic experience.

To my son-in-law, Danton DeMille, thank you for being there for our family during this difficult time.

Thanks to Nathaniel Pope, our Public Relations representative and long-time friend whose powerful advice and actions launched the PR ship.

Special thanks to Eric Flack, Chief Investigative Reporter at WUSA9 for writing the prime-time news narrative "Grandma, Why Are You Here" that received an Emmy Award in 2020.

Thank you to The Honorable Judge Merry

C. Hudson and Attorneys Clinton Evans and Hyacinth Collins whose friendship was like a balm in Gilead and helped us find legal representation.

Heartfelt thanks to Reverend Edward Jackson of Alfred Street Baptist Church, Alexandria, Virginia, who arrived at 5 a.m. to provide emotional and spiritual support when I turned myself in for arrest. He walked this journey with our family all the way through the court process.

To my psychiatrist, Dr. Kathryn Rickard who diagnosed my Post-Traumatic Stress Disorder and helped me cope with crippling fear, mental anguish, and loss of self-esteem.

This book may not have been published without the encouragement and support of Johnnie R. Jackson, PhD who believed my story had so much value to share at this time in US history.

PREFACE

Racism and police brutality are not thinly veiled political concepts. They are the reality that Americans of African descent must live with as unwelcome companions of our daily existence. As common as the air we breathe or the water we drink or the food we eat, we must stay woke to this existential energy to recognize and describe our truth to navigate our environment with clarity to survive. Encountering these realities often results in the need to activate our best friend, JUSTICE.

My husband Eugene and I have walked the earth a total of one-hundred and sixty years. We were born in the Jim Crow South, like our parents who were born in the late 1890's. We share a common set of values stemming from experiences related to racism, discrimination, fear, police cruelty, and white supremacy at its most gripping. The chokehold of this time was false arrests and accusations, harassment, lynching, separate schools, public facilities, communities, churches, beaches, swimming pools, stores, hotels, restaurants, and transportation to name a few. We did not have access to new schoolbooks, or teachers with multiple degrees, or other resources to expand our educational opportunities. But we made it. Through the grace of God, and the strength of our parents, families, and communities we learned how to navigate society without poking the bear.

Both Eugene and I protested Jim Crow laws by participating in sit-ins and marches, attending speeches of Civil Rights leaders such as the Reverend Dr. Martin Luther King, Jr., and working with community and civic leaders help our people achieve their goals. Fortunately, the United States of America has the Constitution and allows us the benefit of basic rights albeit not implemented as equal rights.

However, we leveraged these rights to our benefit. Members of our family including our grandfathers, uncles, brothers, and others served in the military, including my oldest sister who was one of the first African American females accepted to the Women's Army Corp in the 1940's. We learned from each other and pulled each other up towards success using the tools we had, grit, determination, innovation, creativity, and strength while leaning on God.

We both left the Jim Crow south and headed north to attend college, start our careers, marry, and have a family. These are what all human beings desire as basic liberties and rights. The right to life, liberty and the pursuit of happiness which is given to us by our Creator, and which governments are created to protect. These rights are unalienable, which are natural, free, and available to everyone. It's amazing that the Declaration of Independence signed on July 4, 1776, gave us these rights, and African Americans are still fighting for them.

Fast forward to the year 2020, the pandemic

caused by coronavirus, the loss of numerous Americans and people around the world, the shooting of unarmed Black men and women, and the killing of George Floyd and Breonna Taylor by police officers sworn to protect citizens has been difficult for me personally. With each protest and the nightly violence, even within eyeshot of the White House in my hometown of Washington, DC, a rush of memories bloomed back in my mind.

Men and women, Americans of all races, White, Black, Asian, American Indian, carried massive signage quilts emblazoned with messages of social justice, peace, equal rights, calls to end police brutality and racism, and many more. Peaceful protests and marches were held in every state, in multiple cities in the United States and all over the world. This was different. This was global. To put a face to racism and white supremacy using an iPhone to videotape the reality, the pain, the loss of breath, lit a flame of insurrection that I had never seen.

My spirit was devastated by the pain of

police officers taking lives without justification. Black men and women with lives, children, families extinguished so carelessly. I understand society's need for the police. What would we do without the police? Society would be a symphony of fears for safety and security orchestrated by criminals and those who disrupt law and order.

Watching these exploits on the television in our home, tears from memories created not too long ago washed over my face. The pain of an unscrupulous police officer entering our peaceful life still fresh in my spirit. Our lives on several occasions were in the 'zone of danger' where we could have been shot, maimed, or killed in an instant. The wound will never, ever heal. Fortunately, we were not shot or killed, but our lives were altered in ways that are unspeakable. Millions of Black people have had similar experiences. Encountering systemic racism and abuse of power at the hands of police seeking to redress perceived harms created and reported by white people is as old as America itself.

With the television still blaring, my body was transported back to the nightmare of my life involving my own "Karen" before the alter-ego born in 2020 existed. The news was playing, but all I could hear was the jail cell door that closed and locked behind me. A sound that I will never forget. The room went dark as I lost consciousness, and there was a sudden hushed silence in the jail cell that minutes before had been my family room. An unsettlingly quiet crept in like darkness eating up sunlight.

In my spirit, I could see the eyes of the cellmates following my every move. Locking me in their stone-cold stares. I felt trapped. I was. There was no escape. I was in jail. For a fleeting moment it all seemed like a dream. A nightmare really. But it was my reality that rushed back in. Bits and pieces of what brought me there flooded my mind.

Why am I here, really? These questions crowded my thoughts. I struggled to hold back tears, to put it all together. To find answers. But my thoughts were frozen in time. My heart was heavy with sadness. I wanted to say something out loud. To talk to someone, but the eyes of the fellow cellmates remained devoid of any emotion. Their eyes held me at bay. Finally, the cell door opened. I was ordered to leave.

Suddenly I regained consciousness and my eyes opened. The protests on television had expanded all over the world. Just seeing this made me feel free. The world was ready to embrace the reality of racism and police abuse of power, and I could finally speak about our experience to the world. Racism and police abuse of power is real and can happen even to senior citizens. **Now, I can tell our story.**

PART ONE

CHAPTER 1

Summer Flowers

We awakened early on May 14, 2015 and left for breakfast on Pennsylvania Avenue on Capitol Hill in Washington, D.C. Springtime to Gene and I meant beautifying our yard and deck. We were looking forward to a visit from our grandchildren, and we wanted to make it special. Gene laughed, saying that our granddaughter loves the flowers we plant and touches each variety asking, "Grandma, what kind of flower is this one?"

"Gene, maybe we should have baby girl plant a special corner in our garden to get her started growing flowers."

"No, Vash, it will be too late. The weather will be warmer."

"That's true, we better get started now."

We finished our coffee and drove to Gingko Gardens to buy flowers. We parked our black

Mercedes in the parking space directly in front. We had our pen and pad in hand, discussing what we should plant. Gene thought we could plant ground cover, pachysandra rather than flowers under the trees this spring, and just as I objected a woman's car struck my driver's side mirror. She pulled forward and hit the side again. She realized that she hit the mirror.

We exited our vehicles, and she examined the mirror. She tried to push it with her hands cursing, calling it the "f'ing mirror."

"Please do not push the mirror," I said. "It works electronically."

"I can make it move by hand," she said. "You need a different f'ing car."

"We need to exchange insurance information," I said. She agreed and said, "it will take too f'ing long for the police to come."

I gave her our insurance card. She handed hers to me; however, it had expired. She was irritated. She told us her dog had just died, and that her husband left her for another woman. She used profanity nearly every other word.

I said, "I guess your husband did leave you for another woman, and I cannot blame him at all for that."

"Well, he did not leave me for a nigger woman like you," she cursed, before adding, "he does not like Black women."

Later in her sworn deposition, I learned that her dead dog was inside her car, and that she was at Gingko's to buy flowers for his grave.

Gene begged me to call the police and not wait for her insurance company to text her to prove her insurance was current.

She continued to curse, "You people keep your f'ing car in a garage." She swung her right front door open, striking the left front fender of our car and dented it. "Now, I have hit this f'ing car again."

Gene told me again to call the police. Her correct insurance information arrived, and I copied it from her cell phone.

She started leaving and turned back to me and cursed at me again. I told her to just leave, pointing my hand at her. Gene and I were astounded by the incident and could not believe the woman's aggressive behavior. This shook me, so I suggested we postpone shopping for flowers. Gene reminded me that our grandkids would be coming soon. Again, I overruled him and together we decided to go to RIPS restaurant to unwind and eat lunch.

At RIPS, I began to experience anxiety at the thought of having to regurgitate that experience. Gene said I should have called the police, and perhaps we would not have been called a racial epithet that we never wanted to hear again. I sat there quiet, barely touching my lunch.

"I miss you," Gene said. "You are so quiet. Are you praying or just thinking?"

"Both," I responded.

We headed home after lunch and rested all afternoon.

Memories, long buried, are easily resurrected in times like these. Born and raised in the Jim Crow South in 1938, in a little town called Filbert in York County, South Carolina, left me afraid of racism and the use of the N-word. Filbert, South Carolina, consisted of a general store, a one-room post office, and a cotton gin.

I was the ninth child born to Cazetta and Marion Sanders. My little brother Ronnie Shay was the last child. My mother died shortly after his birth. My parents were the bedrock of the community in which we lived. Daddy was a school principal and a minister. Mother was a homemaker. We lived on almost two hundred acres, which was the largest black-owned farm in York County. Even with heavily enforced Jim Crow laws, my daddy gave me the spirit of invincibility and my princess power was in full force.

Both my parents were Christians, and the Bible and its teachings were the foundation and principles of how we were raised. Daddy named all ten of his children from biblical or historical figures. Our parents believed that no matter where we found ourselves or the situations that life presented, we had our name to remind us of who we were and the message that name or figure represented.

I called our daughter Ginger later that evening for our usual evening chat. We always spoke after she returned home from work and finished having dinner with her husband, Danton. The phone rang an unusual number of times, and I was just about to hang up when she answered.

"Hi, Mommy," she said. She knew that it was me because her phone announced callers.

"Hi, darling," I responded.

"How was your day?" she asked.

"Oh my, what a day we had. You are not going to believe this."

"What happened, Mommy? I can tell from your voice that you sound stressed."

We could always tell by our voices what kind of day the other had. I guess that is how it is with mothers and daughters.

"Well, I was involved in an accident today."

"Really? Oh, my goodness, what happened?" she asked.

"Don't get upset," I told her. "We are okay,

but I have never experienced anything like this before, especially not in public. A woman backed into our car in front of Gingko's. She was just so nasty, yelling and cursing at me. She said that her dog had just died and that her husband left her for another woman. Then she called me the N-word."

"What?! No way, you have got to be kidding me."

"No, I am not. Gene told me to call the police because she was so unusually upset and agitated. It was just strange."

"Mommy, you should have called the police. That kind of response is just not normal. You never know what is going on with people."

"You are right. I just thought we could settle it ourselves."

"Well, how did it end?" Ginger asked.

"We ended up exchanging information, but it took a while. Then, after that, she continued to yell at me, and I realized I better not say anything to her to get her more upset. I became afraid that she might hit me, and I didn't want to fall and get hurt."

"Oh, Mommy, I am so sorry that happened to you today."

"Well, we will just put the car in the shop, get the mirror repaired and dent removed, and try to forget about what a horrible experience it was."

"She hit your mirror and dented the car?"

"Yes."

"Wow, well, at least it wasn't worse, and you all didn't get hurt."

"Right."

Ginger and I talked about her day and about the upcoming visit with our grandchildren. *I am glad I can put all this behind me.* At least, I thought.

CHAPTER 2

GETTING THE MAIL

I did not sleep well that evening. I tossed and turned most of the night. The experience at Gingko's flower shop was probably the cause. Now that I was older, I had trouble sleeping when an issue sat in my spirit that caused me stress, or that I could not resolve. I could still hear her calling me the N-word. It was so degrading to listen to that word directed towards me.

Having grown up when the N-word was as common as using the word 'and,' my father always taught us how to handle situations like that. "Vashti," he would say, "if anyone ever calls you out of your name, don't say a word back to them. Just look straight ahead and remain silent. Words cannot hurt you."

Despite my father's advice, words can and do hurt. Particularly this word. This word cuts through the air like a knife used to serve up a slice of white supremacy or bounces out in a conversation between black people to invoke feelings that only we can wink and nod to each other in agreement about its meaning. But mostly, it brings back memories of the pain, destruction, and shame that I remember hearing about as a young child, talking to my brother Ronnie as we explored the woods on our farm.

Long ago, when I was nine, we were walking to school and I asked him what happened to my best friend Cora Belle. The Reeds had thirteen children and owned their home that was on an acre of land. They were farmers. I attended school in Filbert with many of their children. We were close friends, practically growing up together.

Sam Reed worked for Mr. Rhodes, who owned a lot of land. Mr. Reed, in his spare time, took care of Mr. Rhodes' yard at his residence. Mrs. Rhodes became angry when Mr. Reed failed to get her flower beds the way she liked them. Sam was called a nigger.

Mr. Reed returned the insult. I guess he just had had enough. He should have known better, but he responded anyway. In the evening, the Ku Klux Klan showed up with a cross and stood it up in his yard, then burned it. Mr. Reed was ordered to leave by morning or get killed. The entire family left their home and all their belongings.

This was a painful time for me. I lost my best friends that I enjoyed playing softball with and doing things country kids do for fun. The school bus was half empty after the Reed kids left. For many years growing up, only my older sisters, brothers, and parents knew the location where they moved.

I was a young girl when I learned about people in a group called the KKK. My daddy explained to all of us that the KKK hated Negro people and did not want us to 'step out of line.' He told us that we needed to not talk back to white people, to mind our own business, and to never go anywhere without telling him or our stepmother. This was life growing up in the Jim Crow South.

The next day after the incident at Gingko's, there was a business card from Detective Phillip McHugh from the Metropolitan Police Department in Washington in our mailbox. The back of the card read, "Call me, Vashti Sherrod," and listed his phone number.

I showed the card to Gene and said, "What could this be about?" I called many times and left messages. He did not return my call until several days later.

When I answered the phone, Detective McHugh said. "Hello, is this Vashti Sherrod?"

I said, "Yes, it is."

"I am Detective McHugh," he stated, "and I left a card in your mailbox to call me. I was in training and unable to return your phone calls. I am calling because I am investigating a report that you assaulted a lady with a gun at Gingko's Flower Shop on Capitol Hill."

Stunned by this accusation, I was in complete shock. "That is not true," I told him.

"I have the video of the incident at the prosecutor's office in DC that shows you brandishing a gun," he said.

Gene could hear the conversation over the phone from where he was sitting. "Good, good, they have a video," he shouted. "Then there's nothing to talk about."

I could tell this angered Detective McHugh because he responded louder, "Where is your car right now? I can search it, take it, and arrest you."

I did not know what to say. I was truly baffled. I responded by saying, "Detective McHugh, we are getting ready to go to York, South Carolina, because my sister had recently died. I will contact you as soon as we return."

"Okay," he said, "I will wait for your call."

"Thank you, goodbye." I ended the call and turned to look at Gene. I could not believe my ears. Buying flowers on Capitol Hill had turned into me being accused of assaulting a woman with a gun. Surely, this was all a mistake, and Detective McHugh would do the appropriate investigation and realize there was no gun on the video.

We headed to South Carolina, and I did not

give the whole thing another thought. I figured it was all a mistake and would get cleared up. While we were on our way South, which triggers special memories, I began to think about my family and my sister who had just died.

Virginia Dare was the first woman born in the 'new world,' and the name of my oldest sister who died almost one year before my encounter in front of Gingko's flower shop. Born in 1920, she was my parent's first child. Their gift from God, they chose to give her this name to always convey the message to her, to "dare to be the first." And she was. She was beautiful, smart, talented, courageous, and determined. After our mother died, my sister helped raise her brothers and sisters until my father remarried.

Virginia was a visionary. She joined the Women's Army Corp in 1943, later attended the historically Black college, Storer College, and retired the Dean of Graduate Admissions at American University in Washington, DC. I was enormously proud to be her little sister.

We returned from South Carolina safely. Much later, we found out that our car could have been impounded, searched, and a warrant for both of us to be jailed anywhere in the United States. Detective McHugh used the WALES police monitoring system and registered our vehicle as having been involved in a crime. God's mercy had been with us, and angels were protecting us. We might not have been safe otherwise. If we had been stopped out of state, I now know we could have never recovered from that.

Eventually, we realized Detective McHugh was aggressively pursuing this false accusation. We knew there was no evidence of a gun on the video because I did not have one. I have never owned or handled a gun. I am afraid of them.

CHAPTER 3

Capitol Hill Stop

It was pouring rain in Mitchellville, Maryland. Gene wondered if we should postpone driving to Euro Motorcars in Bethesda, Maryland, to have our car serviced. I told Gene that we should deal with the rain because appointments are too difficult to reschedule, so we decided to make the trip.

Once there, we turned in the car and relaxed in the customer lounge, reading the newspapers, drinking coffee, eating their great muffins, and chatting with others who were waiting as well. The service was completed, and we decided to drive to our cleaners on Capitol Hill to pick up laundry and dry cleaning.

It was great to drive past the Smithsonian, Air and Space Museum, the Hirshhorn, and the new National Museum for the American

Indian. All these museums are located on or near Independence Avenue, Northwest. I worked for the Smithsonian for many years, starting in the "Castle," where the institution's founder James Smithson is buried. At that time, there was not a museum dedicated to African American history, but thankfully now, there is a beautiful edifice memorializing our history.

As we approached Pennsylvania Avenue and the intersection of Independence in Southwest, I heard loud voices shouting, "Stop the car! Stop the car!" Immediately I stopped the car and looked in my rearview mirror. Horrified, I was scared to death of what I saw.

Three Capitol Hill police officers each held large black shotguns pointed directly at our heads. "Gene, Gene, get down," I screamed. "There are guns pointed at our heads!" I had already placed my head on the steering wheel. Gene placed his on the dashboard. One of the officers appeared at my window and the other at Gene's window. They lowered their shot guns and anchored them by their sides propping them on the ground. I was crying and visibly upset.

The officer said to me, "I am not going to arrest any senior citizens." His soft, warm words were low key and calming for both of us. Interestingly enough, he did not initially ask us for our ID or registration. He was more interested in finding out if someone else could have driven the car or if it was possible the car had been stolen. Our answer was an emphatic no.

"Where have you all been today?" he asked.

I showed him a bottle of water with the "Euro Motorcars" label inscribed on it.

"Where is that?" he asked.

I explained that Euro Motorcars was a Mercedes Benz dealership in Bethesda, Maryland.

He said, "Well I am not from this area, so I do not know where that is."

I did not know why we were stopped, and we were too afraid to ask him. He asked for our ID, insurance card and registration. Then he said, "Allegedly our system shows that this car has been involved in criminal activity. Sit tight, stay calm, and I will be right back."

Upon his return, he told us that another officer was on his way to talk to us.

About an hour passed before Detective Phillip McHugh arrived and ordered us out of our vehicle. The detective harassed us. With a mocking laugh, he said with sarcasm, "Remember me?" Then he presented a search warrant for me to sign. He said, "If you do not sign, I will take your car." Feeling threatened by him, I immediately signed the search warrant.

Many people had gathered around the Sam Rayburn government building. Detective McHugh searched the car inside and out. We could hear the onlookers remarking, giving their opinions to each other. They were offering words of support to us, possibly because of our age, and seeing that we were visibly shaken. They also spoke of Gene's being visually impaired. One of the Capitol Hill police observed that he had already misjudged the distance between the car and the street curb and remained by his side to assist him.

The search ended and no gun was found. Detective McHugh never returned our ID and personal information, and I was too afraid to ask for it. The detective requested that I follow him to his office, and my answer was no I vehemently objected, telling him that my attorney would need to accompany us.

An onlooker heard Gene when he told me that we should still stop by our cleaners which was one block away. We headed to the cleaners. I went in and one of the onlookers ran to meet us there. She showed her support in the cleaners and reached out to us, tearing the top portion of her check off that not only provided her name and address, but most importantly her phone number. By providing us with her personal information, Sharon became an important witness for our case against Detective McHugh.

We decided to call Ginger to share what happened with the Capitol Hill police and Detective McHugh. Her phone rang and rang, so we became worried. Ginger finally answered, and I told her that she could never in her wildest imagination guess what happened to us.

"Tell me, Mother, and get to the point," she said. "Your voice is trembling, and Dad is saying something in the background that does not sound palatable. Just get to it," she said, raising her voice which rarely she does.

Gene told me to pull the car over so that we could talk. We told Ginger everything that happened from Euro Motorcars to the guns being pointed at us to Detective McHugh's appearance.

We arrived back home, exhausted, and nervous, feeling we needed to pray for our safety and to ask God why this was happening to us.

The telephone rang, and it was Ginger. "Just letting you know that I am on the way. I told Danton what happened and that I would be home late. He was devastated about it and told me to tell you everything will be okay." Ginger left work and drove to our home to comfort us. Her being with us was just what the doctor ordered.

I felt sad knowing that it must have shocked Danton to hear about our experience. My son-in-law is a truly kind, gentle person. He is also Caucasian, so I could not even imagine what he must have thought about the situation.

We had talked about social injustice and racism as a family many times, particularly about recent events that have occurred in the news with police. Never did we imagine anyone in our family would be a victim.

Ginger arrived about fifteen minutes later. I could see her walking quickly to the door. She spent most of the evening consoling us. We talked about what steps should be taken to prevent Detective McHugh from hurting us. She spoke about our safety and encouraged us to begin the search for an attorney for legal advice.

Gene and I immediately reached out to various attorneys that we knew. It was time. We needed their help and could no longer handle Detective McHugh and whatever he was up to.

CHAPTER 4

THE RAID AT LAKE FRONT

On July 7th, just two days after our grandchildren left to go back home, we were tormented by Detective McHugh again. The day started out like any normal day. We were still catching up on our rest and did not have plans to go out. The plan was to get up, have breakfast, read the newspaper, watch a little TV, catch up with friends, take a walk in the garden, and then have an early dinner. Little did we know what would befall us on that ordinary summer day.

At approximately 9 p.m., Gene and I retired to our bedroom for the evening. We were in bed relaxing, listening to TV. Though not asleep totally, we were beginning to drift toward sleep when I heard the faint sound of the doorbell in the background.

Having raised children, I am attuned to

slight noises. I thought I heard it again and was curious. "Gene, I wonder who is ringing the doorbell this time of evening?"

He listened and heard it as well.

We were not expecting any guests or visitors, so we dismissed it. I thought probably it was someone selling something, or someone who had the wrong house. Suddenly the faint ringing of the doorbell stopped.

"Good, I think they are gone," I said.

Shortly after, we both heard pounding on the door from our deck. Now, we were more awake, wondering what in the world was going on. It was so unusual we became anxious. I looked up at the alarm panel, which was right at the door inside our bedroom and noticed that it was off. I tried to activate the emergency on the alarm and discovered, strangely enough, it was not working.

"Gene, the alarm isn't working!"

"What? I don't understand why it wouldn't be working, just try again," he replied.

So, I tried again. It still did not work. The banging on the backdoor got louder. I looked down the hall of our home, which leads to the other rooms and saw flashing lights. Gene told me the weather report had said it was a storm coming up and maybe it was thunder. We relaxed again, until the banging continued. We were terrified and thought for sure this was a home invasion, one like we experienced at our previous residence in Washington, DC.

I had a flashback to twenty years ago when our house was broken into. It happened extremely fast. We heard knocks on the front door that lasted about fifteen minutes. I was on the phone talking to my girlfriend Constance, who was my best friend in high school. We have been friends for over sixty years. In the middle of our conversation, I heard a sudden, grand, large boom and then a second boom. "Constance, someone just broke into our house," I screamed! I ran to the alarm pad to turn it on, but it did not come on because a door was already open. But the alarm made a loud beeping sound, which probably caused the burglars to run away. Constance called the police, and they were there in minutes with weapons drawn and blaring sirens going off. We stayed upstairs in the locked bedroom until they made their way upstairs, saying, "Police, police." We learned later that the burglars had kicked in a downstairs basement door and had already started going through desks. I guess the alarm beeping scared them off. Thank God, we were saved.

"Gene, do you think someone is trying to break in the house?"

He did not respond. We cowered in the bed, hoping what we were hearing was something going on in our neighbor's backyard.

I was too afraid to look out the window because if it were a break-in, they would see me. I would have called the police, but our phone was in the library across from our bedroom. I remove it from our bedroom at night because I do not want it to wake me up. Ginger always pleads with me to keep the phone in our bedroom at night no matter what. All Gene and I could do was discuss what we could do if our house was indeed being broken into. I told Gene that I was going to jump out of the window.

Unlike before, this time we had no one to call the police for us, so all we could do was think about where we could hide. Then boom. Finally, we heard the same sound of the door being kicked in.

"Vash, we are being robbed!"

Then we heard, "Police, police, come downstairs with your hands up!"

We obeyed, but in a state of shock where we could not even speak. We were both in our pajamas. I, in a short gown, with no sleeves. My arms out, hair was undone, no makeup, nothing. No one in the world had seen me in that state except my husband and my daughter. I felt so ashamed, humiliated, and violated physically, emotionally, and spiritually.

There was Detective McHugh and about six officers from Prince George's County and Bowie Police with guns drawn at us as we came downstairs with our hands up. Detective McHugh smiled at me and said sheepishly, "remember me." I did not reply. Gene was immediately taken and handcuffed with his hands behind his back. I was ordered to place my hands on my head.

"What is this all about? What is going on?" we asked. But no one answered our questions. We were ordered to "give up the firearm and bullets."

"Go get the gun and bullets!" They shouted at us.

"We don't have a gun or bullets in our home. We have never owned a firearm or bullets," we said.

Then Detective McHugh said, "The search is on."

We were instructed to sit in the living room on an antique Victorian red-velvet loveseat that is a family heirloom from Gene's mother as they tore apart our home looking for a gun.

Two police officers stayed with us in the living room with one sitting on one of our French Bergère chairs.

They searched our house for at least an hour and thirty minutes, including our garage and vehicles parked on our pad. Huddled together in disbelief, we watched police officers from three departments ransack our home.

One female officer approached me about how I was dressed. "Ma'am, would you like me to go upstairs and get something for you to cover yourself up in?"

"Yes, please," I responded.

"Okay," she said. She left and went upstairs but came back shortly with nothing. "Mrs. Sherrod, I'm sorry, but Detective McHugh was in your closet conducting the search so I could not enter your bedroom."

As the officers completed each room, they convened outside and spoke with Detective McHugh. One of them came back into the house and had us sign a document. To this day, I do not even know what it was. But I was not going to ask any questions.

"Mr. and Mrs. Sherrod, we did not find any weapons or ammunition. I am the supervisor of the search, and I will document it accordingly," the officer said.

Gene said, "Thanks," but I did not say a word.

All night long, we huddled together on the sofa in our family room with the door breached, unlocked and unsecured. We felt numb, sad, and angry. Crying intermittently while holding hands off and on. Gene and I have suffered significant medical and health challenges, the loss of loved ones, and life in general. But nothing compared to this. Having taken so much pride in our home, I could not even look at it. I kept my eyes fixed ahead and never looked around the house that night. We were so devastated that we could not pour a glass of water.

We were counting the minutes until we could call Ginger with the news. We did not want to call her that evening for fear she would race over to our house in the dark and risk getting into an accident. It would not be safe for her and Danton to drive upset like that.

When morning came, we had not slept all night. I called Ginger. "Hi, Ginny," which was a name I sometimes called her.

"Good morning, Mommy, how are you?"

Barely getting my breath, I uttered, "I am okay."

Immediately her radar went up. "What's the matter, Mother?" she asked.

Still in shock, I was speechless. "Nothing, I'm okay."

"There's something wrong, Mommy. What is the matter?"

But I could not muster a word. I just could not put into words what we had endured. And I did not want to tell her because she would have been hysterical and then driven to our home in that state.

Then she said, "Mommy, there is something wrong. Do you want me to come there this morning?"

"Yes," I replied. That was all I needed to say. The mother-daughter bond kicked in with just one word. Our daughter to the rescue.

I could see her when she walked up on the porch. She walked into the house and looked at us. Devastated by the disarray, she fell on the floor and started screaming at the top of her lungs.

Thinking we needed medical attention, Ginger told us to get dressed.

Gene said, "Pretty baby, we do not need to get dressed for medical care."

Ginger returned to her car to get her phone and photographed the house while we sat there, speechless and traumatized. Later that day, she employed a cleaning company for support and started looking for a company to repair the door.

The next day a friend of ours called asking, "What the hell happened in there last night?" Apparently, she knew the neighbor who lived across the street from us. She told me our neighbors watched and saw everything. We were under siege and did not see the street closed with the SWAT team from Prince George County on our block.

Following the raid on our home, whenever we left the house in our car, we could see how differently our neighbors treated us. Gone were the hellos and waves. Now we endured head turns and downward glances. This hurt us in our hearts.

Some nights I would peer through the front window when I could not sleep trying to guess what our neighbors could be thinking about us. Perhaps they thought we were drug dealers, thieves, or participants of some other illegal activity happening in our home.

With three different police jurisdictions raiding our home, it certainly looked like some terrible illegal activity was happening at 920. Our foreheads were branded with the mark of "C" for criminals.

CHAPTER 5

FRIENDS IN THE LAW

The day after the raid, our house was still open to anyone who wanted to walk in. We were able to lock the screen, but the front door was demolished. The hinges were hanging down so that anyone driving past the house could see that the door was damaged.

We felt so unsafe that we moved downstairs into the basement at night because we were scared to sleep upstairs. Danton and Ginger did their best to secure the front door. They begged us to leave the house immediately and stay with them, but with our house unsecured, we could not. They stayed with us while we sought someone to repair the door frame and locks. We found a contractor, but unfortunately, we had to wait a week for him to complete the significant number of repairs.

When we realized the gravity of the legal

quicksand we had found ourselves sinking into, Gene called a dear family friend, Attorney Clinton Hawthorne.

Gene met Clinton when he was a young kid growing up in Portsmouth, Virginia, where Gene is from. The older children in the Sherrod and Hawthorne family went to school together. They also lived in the same neighborhood, and in the '50s, Black families were remarkably close to one another.

Segregated schools and churches contributed to that closeness. We had to support one another, help one another when needed, and have fun and party with one another. Life was hard for Blacks, but we made the burden light in our communities, which gave us the spirit to go on despite being despised by white people.

The Sherrods and Hawthornes were college-educated and many of them attended historically Black colleges and universities (HBCU), specifically Norfolk State in Virginia, or Howard University in Washington, DC.

Gene went to Norfolk State, and then did something different by attending the University of Maryland (U of M) in College Park, Maryland. U of M is not an HBCU, it is a state college with approximately 200 black students out of several thousand. However, the relationships built while attending HBCUs and making lifelong friends in fraternities and sororities kept us in a strong network of professionals we could call on when necessary.

Gene majored in architecture and initially became a teacher. His dream was to start a construction company, which he did with a longtime friend from Portsmouth. We call our friendship "the Portsmouth Connection." Even to this day, we've kept in touch with friends from college and from our respective hometowns.

Eventually, Gene started his own construction company and worked on significant projects in the District, such as the Watergate Building, the Robert F. Kennedy Stadium, Bates Street Redevelopment Project under Mayor Marion Barry, and major mall construction projects such as Iverson and Landover Malls.

Still in disbelief that the simple act of going to buy summer flowers had propelled us deeper into a trap set by Detective McHugh to satisfy his need to wield power and to come to the aid of a white woman in distress, we waited for Clinton's return call.

When the phone rang, Gene answered. "Man, I've been waiting on this call."

"Hey, man, how are you all doing? I got your call, but I have been on a case and got tied up. I'm sorry for the delay."

"That's okay," Gene said. "You aren't going to believe what has happened to Vash and me. Well, it is a long story, but we need a criminal attorney."

"A criminal attorney? For what?"

"Well, a lady hit our car on Capitol Hill, and she called the police and told them Vash assaulted her with a semiautomatic weapon."

"Oh, my goodness, that is ridiculous!"

"Well, yes, it is. Vash didn't have a gun.

She's never had a gun, and the detective said there was a video of the whole incident."

"Wait, Gene, did you say there was a video?"

"Yes, there was a video."

"Well, that's good."

"Obviously, the detective didn't look at it."

"Let me make a few calls, and I will get back to you quickly."

"Thanks, man, I appreciate it."

"You are welcome, Gene. Tell Vash that everything is going to be alright."

"Okay, I will. Bye."

Clinton Hawthorne called again later with good news. "Gene, I have an attorney who can help you with this matter. He is a great criminal attorney; his name is Brian McDaniel, a friend of mine and frat brother from Howard University law school. He will call you within the hour.

"Clinton, you have made my day," Gene said.

Within the hour Attorney McDaniel called

us. Gene told him, "We have a story to tell you."

He responded, "I know I can help you just show up in my office at 10 a.m. tomorrow. I am located on K Street in DC."

"What a relief," Gene said. "My wife is scared to death."

Eternally grateful for the help of friends, we prayed that everything would work out for us.

While waiting to hear from Clinton, we also reached out to our dear friend of forty years, Mary Chisum. Mary is a retired judge from the State of Maryland court system who now had her own law firm. She and Gene met years earlier as neighbors in Silver Spring, Maryland.

At the time, Mary was a law school student attending Howard Law School, and her husband Robert was attending Howard's medical school. Bob, as we called him, eventually became a successful pediatrician and an acclaimed pediatric neurosurgeon at Washington Hospital Center with his own practice in Washington, DC. He was a dear man and a great friend who passed from an exceedingly long illness the same year all this happened.

Bob and Mary were our favorite couple to socialize with in the Washington, DC social scene. We interacted socially in each other's homes with many of our friends who were high-powered entrepreneurs or professionals in law, medicine, and the political arena. Every year we attended annual balls, social gatherings of alumnae organizations, and events sponsored by social groups such as the Links, the Washington, DC Society of Medical Professionals, the Association of Black Legal Professionals, the National Urban League, and the Congressional Black Caucus. Mary and I would plan our attire for a week and could not wait to see each other in full after-five regalia. We often rented limousines and made a weekend out of it by staying in the sponsors' hotel.

"Mary, this is Gene."

"Hey, Gene, how are you doing? I have been thinking about calling you all."

"You must have been reading my mind."

"Stevie was just saying, 'where in the world is my Uncle Gene.' How is Vash?"

"Well, that is why I am calling. She is not doing well. Neither am I."

"What, Gene? I am so sorry to hear that. What is wrong?"

"Well, Mary, we had an accident on Capitol Hill, and the lady who hit our car reported to the police that Vash pulled a gun out on her."

"What? No, you are kidding me, Gene." Mary was distraught. She could hardly catch her breath. She was still dealing with the stress of losing her husband.

"Gene, you need a criminal attorney right away. You know that I don't do that kind of law, but I can refer you to a couple of lawyers who can help you."

Mary gave us the names of two law firms, one in Rockville and the other in downtown DC on Seventh Street.

Attorney McDaniel's office was not far from K Street. Gene and I were escorted to a lovely conference room to wait for him to arrive for the meeting. I was a basket case. I had not really slept since the raid or eaten much food. I felt weak, the stress of it was getting to me. I was crying a lot and just a mess. Thankfully, Gene was so supportive.

Just as Attorney McDaniel walked into the conference room, Gene grabbed my hand and squeezed it tight. I took a deep breath and lifted my head and eyes up. I gazed upon Attorney McDaniel as he walked into the room with his plaid suit, pressed white shirt, and beige tie.

It was the middle of July and scorching hot outside, but he was appropriately dressed for his profession. Brown skin and eyes with curly closed-cut hair, he was young, maybe forty-five years old. He reminded me of our son.

"Good morning, Mr. and Mrs. Sherrod," he said. "I am Attorney McDaniel. I understand that I was referred to you by Attorney Clinton Hawthorne, my frat brother."

I blacked out all the cordialities. Gene took it over. As I listened to them talk, all I could think was, *I cannot believe that I am here.* About five minutes or so passed, and he said, "Mrs. Sherrod, tell me what happened."

I shared what happened at Gingko's flower shop, followed by the Capitol Hill stop, and then the raid. He listened intently without any questions, and I saw him take a few notes. He said, "You said there was a video?"

I said, "Yes."

The meeting did not last long, but I felt amazingly comfortable with him by the end of it.

He had an easy-going approach for a lawyer. He shared with us that he was from Seattle, Washington, which explained it. He was not a native Washingtonian, which was not bad, but different.

I started to cry a bit. My nerves were shot.

"Mrs. Sherrod," he said, "you are going to be okay. I understand that this is difficult for you. It is a new experience for you, but I promise you, you are going to be okay,"

"Okay," I said. "I hope so. It is just so unfair and wrong. That lady is lying."

I reiterated that I did not have a gun and did

not threaten her at all. "She was threatening me. I was afraid of her. Gene told me to call the police, but I did not listen to him. I just wanted to hurry up so I could get back to Bowie. I cannot believe that buying flowers for our deck has ended up having to retain a criminal attorney to represent me."

Attorney McDaniel said, "Well, I'm not sure what is totally needed, but it appears that they are going to file charges if they haven't already based on the steps they have taken to date."

I looked at him in disbelief and said. "Even though they don't have a video without a gun on it?"

"Well, they can still make charges based on what the claimant has told them. They have to investigate it fairly and without bias."

"Well, you said the magic words— 'without bias,' which is what the problem is going to be."

"Yes," he said, "we have this problem that is difficult, and I hate to say it, but African Americans are charged with crimes by Whites every day without any evidence." He shuffled some papers. "Well, let me tell you about my retainer." He reviewed all the details of his retainer for our consideration. Fortunately, we had the money at the rate he quoted, which was enough to enjoy a seven-day vacation in a five-star hotel in Hawaii.

"I will have my assistant bring you a copy of the Retainer Agreement so that you can review it tonight. Mr. and Mrs. Sherrod, it would be an honor to represent you to ensure that your constitutional rights are protected and that you receive fairness and protection from further harassment under the law. Please call me if you have any questions."

We stood up and shook his hand, thanking him.

As we were leaving, we realized that we still needed to meet with the attorneys Mary referred us to. She had contacted each of them directly, so we owed it to her to follow-up as promised. As soon as I got in the car, I called each attorney. I was able to get an appointment the next day with each firm. It was going to be a busy day.

Since we were downtown already, we decided to have lunch at the Prime Rib restaurant on K Street. We walked into the restaurant, and the maître d Larry greeted us. "Good afternoon, Mr. and Mrs. Sherrod, good to see you again."

"Hi, Larry," I said, it's good to see you too."

"Come on in," he said, "your table is ready."

We did not need to make a reservation at the Prime Rib. It was like going home. Our favorite table was available, so he knew to take us there. Many years ago, Gene had an office on K Street, and the Prime Rib became his favorite restaurant. We dined here for family celebrations, birthdays, anniversaries, holidays, and lunch.

The kids have gotten a bit tired of it, but now that they are older, they appreciate and respect our family's thirty-plus year tradition.

It was consoling and comforting to be in a place where we were recognized and our reputation was intact. Memories of many joyous and happy moments shared over many occasions revived my spirit and belief that we would be alright. We had worked too hard and given too much to not be.

"Good morning, Vash, it is time to get up. We have an appointment with the other lawyers today."

"Gene, I don't feel well, maybe we should reschedule. I think my pressure is up. I better take it."

I took my pressure, and it was high. So, I decided to lay down for another hour with the hope that it would go down. Taking it an hour later gave me solace, it was better. So, I readied myself to face meeting more attorneys. We needed help, and God had sent us friends to help us plant the seeds we needed.

The drive to Rockville took forty-five minutes. The day was sunny but not hot. Rockville was well known to us, I went to the spa and shopped at Saks Fifth Avenue and Mazza Galleria for many years. Several of my doctors were also in this area. But the most significant sentiment I held for the area was my sister Virginia lived here for many years after leaving Southwest Washington, DC. She lived in an exclusive community called The Crest of the Wickford across from White Flint Mall. When she moved there, she and her husband were the only African Americans living there. We were so proud of her.

Upon entering this firm, we did not feel the same way that we did upon entering McDaniel's office. It was much smaller, but because Mary referred us, I knew she had great respect for their capabilities.

We met with Attorney Smith, who had more experience in personal injury law than criminal law, but he told us that he had another attorney who focused on criminal law. We told him everything that had happened to us from beginning to end. He was sympathetic and emotive about how our constitutional rights were violated and assured us there was no probable cause to bring charges. He based his opinion on the fact that Detective McHugh could not have seen a gun on the video.

Neither of us had seen the video, but we all knew there was no gun. He was a wise lawyer and took into consideration the fact that we were over seventy years old and homeowners without a criminal record.

He could not believe a police officer would file charges on us based on our profile. We discussed his retainer and what he needed to take the case.

His highest and immediate interest was to get publicity for what had happened to us. Gene and I were a little leery about that because we were not sure about the impact going to press would have on our case. We were also deathly afraid of Detective McHugh and what he could do to us.

Grateful for the referral, we thanked him for his time.

We walked out discussing Mary and how helpful she had been. These meetings gave us a chance to present our case, get an opinion, and learn more about how we should approach the situation. We came away with several benefits to the meeting but agreed that

Clinton's referral was the best so far. We still had one more referral, but we were able to rule out the last one.

Heading to 7th Street in downtown DC from Rockville was tedious. It was lunchtime, so there was a lot of traffic. We decided to pick up a sandwich on the way and eat in the car. Finally, we got in front of the building and were lucky to find parking right in front. This firm was Jones and Smith, and our friend Mary knew the leading partner Samuel Jones. She worked with him years before becoming a judge and had kept in touch ever since.

As we entered the firm's lobby, a photo of him was on the wall leading to the elevator.

When we got off the elevator, a young woman was waiting. "Mr. and Mrs. Sherrod?" she asked.

"Yes," I responded.

"Welcome to Jones and Smith. My name is Sarah, and I am going to escort you to our conference room."

Gene and I glanced at each other. We followed her as she led us through huge mahogany doors. Two people were sitting at a huge conference table large enough to seat fifty people. Both individuals stood and introduced themselves.

They were both attorneys, but neither was Samuel Jones.

"Thank you for coming, Mr. and Mrs. Sherrod. I am Walter Rhodes, and this is my colleague Lori Sanchez."

We all shook hands and sat down. The purpose of the introductory meeting was for these two attorneys to get the facts before the leading partner joined us.

We talked for about an hour with them taking meticulous notes before Attorney Jones joined us, along with a well-known criminal lawyer we cannot name. (Apparently, Jones and Smith partners with other high-powered firms when they feel a prospective case warrants it.) They were both relaxed and asked us to give a quick overview of what happened and why we were there. The other attorneys quickly filled in the blanks, and both mentioned that our constitutional rights were severely compromised.

At the end of the meeting, they shared what their retainer agreement would be, which was quite different than Attorney McDaniel's. We had to pay for all costs, including postage, copying, etc., in addition to the flat fee, which was a lot higher.

We were okay with it until we got a funny feeling from them at the end as they escorted us from the conference room. The criminal attorney joked, "Mr. Sherrod, you forgot your gun in the conference room."

They laughed, but we didn't think it was funny. We said our goodbyes and left the building. As soon as we got in the car, we agreed that Attorney McDaniel was the best criminal lawyer to represent me.

We called Attorney McDaniel that evening and told him that we wanted to execute the retainer agreement. As part of the terms, we had to provide one-third of the total fees with two other installments due in ninety days until fully paid. We scheduled an appointment for the end of the week and decided to call Attorney Jones to let him know that we would not need his services.

"Hello, Mrs. Sherrod."

Yes, Attorney Jones. I wanted to let you know that we have selected another firm."

"Oh well, that is okay, but I did want you to know that we called the court as we have a lot of contacts there. Did you know that there is a warrant out for your arrest?"

I gasped, and my throat locked up, so speaking was not possible.

He continued, "You are going to need to turn yourself in to MPD on Indiana Avenue. I advise that you do it as soon as possible without delay. If you don't, you might be arrested anywhere once they begin to look for you. Also, this case will cost you a lot more money than we quoted you today."

My chest began to ache.

Gene was asking me, "What is he telling you?"

Later he told me my face contorted and

turned ashy gray. I was borderline having a heart attack.

Tears streamed down my face as the harsh reality settled in. I ended the call with Attorney Jones and told Gene what he said. Gene called Attorney McDaniel to tell him about the arrest warrant, and he advised us to come to his office in the morning to discuss turning myself in.

SUPERIOR COURT OF THE DISTRICT OF COLUMBIA
CRIMINAL DIVISION

COMPLAINT

DCTN: U15017952
Lockup No: 38
Case No: 2015 CW 2437

District of Columbia ss:

Defendant's Name: Vashti Valma Sherrod (First) (MI) (Last) (PDID) 15070009 (CCNO)

Also Known As: (First) (Middle) (Last)

Address: 920 Lake Front Drive, Mitchellville, MD

On or about May 14, 2015, within the District of Columbia, Vashti Valma Sherrod assaulted Diane Schulz with a dangerous weapon, that is, gun. **(Assault with a Dangerous Weapon, in violation of 22 D.C. Code, Section 402 (2001 ed.))**

Co-Defendants:

2015 JUL 10 PM 2 12
FILED

Inv [signature]
Affiant's Name McHugh

Subscribed and sworn to before me this 10 day of July, 2015

[signature]
(Judge) (Deputy Clerk)

WARRANT

To The United States Marshal or any other authorized federal officer or the Chief of Police of the District of Columbia:

WHEREAS the foregoing complaint and affidavit supporting the allegations thereof have been submitted, and there appearing probable cause and reasonable grounds for the issuance of an arrest warrant for Vashti Valma Sherrod

YOU ARE THEREFORE COMMANDED TO BRING THE DEFENDANT BEFORE SAID COURT OR OTHER PERSON ENUMERATED IN 18 U.S.C. 3041 forthwith to answer said charge.

Issued July 10, 2015 [signature] Superior Court of the District of Columbia

Title 16: ☐ Rule 105: ☐ Judge:

Sex: Female	DOB: 09/17/1938	CCN: 15070009	PDID:
Papering Officer: Mchugh			Badge No.: IV1755
T100230 OFFICER MUST EXECUTE RETURN			
Officer's Name: [signature]			Date / Time: July 10, 2015
AUSA Signature: [signature]			Fel. I ☐ AFTC ☐ Fel. II ☒

1. This affidavit in support of an arrest warrant is a summary of the investigation of this offense, which included several interviews and investigative steps. This affidavit is not a verbatim record of those interviews, nor does it detail every step of the investigation; rather, it provides an overview of the case. Your affiant in this matter is Investigator Phillip J. McHugh, of the Metropolitan Police Department's Criminal
Investigations Division.

2. Of May 14, 2015, Complaining Witness 1 (CW) contacted the Metropolitan Police Department and reported that she was threatened and assaulted with a firearm in the 900 block of 11th Street SE, Washington DC. The offense was documented with case number 2015-070-009. Investigator McHugh was assigned as the lead investigator on the case for the First District Detectives Unit

3. On May 14, 2015 at approximately 1110 hours, CW was attempting to parallel-park in front of a flower shop located at 911 11th Street SE DC. A black Mercedes Benz sedan bearing Maryland tag HJF502 was parked on the side of the road directly in front of the flower shop. While backing to park, CW accidently crashed In the side mirror of the Mercedes. CW reported that the female driver of the Mercedes, subsequently identified as VASHTI VALMA SHERROD, immediately began screaming and cursing at CW because of minordamage CW had caused.

4. CW exited her car to inspect the damage and begin exchanging insurance information. SHERROD and her m le front seat passenger, subsequently identified as her husband Eugene, both exited the Mercedes and inspected the damaged mirror. The group argued over the extent of the damage and whether the damage was pr existing or caused by the crash. The argument escalated when SHERROD began making racial comments and disparaging remarks about CW's appearance and dress.

5. CW asked SHERROD to provide her documents so that they could exchange information for their insurance companies. SHERROD refused to provide her license or registration, only giving CW her insurance card.

6. A er writing down the insurance information, CW again asked for SHERROD's name, to which SHERROD re lied, "I'm not going to give you my name. I'm going to give you the barrel of my gun." At that time, E gene Sherrod encouraged his wife by saying, "Yeah yeah, get it, get it." CW did not take this threat seriously at first because the Sherrod's both appeared to be in their 80s. However, VASHTI SHERROD went to her car and reached under the driver's seat, pulling out what CW described as a black semi-automatic pistol similar to what a police officer would carry. CW reported that Vashti Sherrod pointed the pistol at her an began walking toward her in a threatening manner. CW walked to the rear of her own car, heading to the driver's side to get away from SHERROD, who followed her to the back of the car. CW got in her car and
left the scene.

7. CW was shown a photograph of the suspect Mercedes from the License Plate Reader system, which she identified as the suspect vehicle. Additionally, Investigator McHugh located video surveillance footage that captured the lengthy interaction, which lasted approximately 17 minutes. The video corroborates CW's series of events. The video shows SHERROD bend down at the driver's seat of her Mercedes and emerge with her right arm raised as if pointing something at CW. SHERROD walks toward CW, who then abruptly reenters he vehicle and leaves the scene. The video quality is not clear enough to see what SHERROD has inher hand, but CW described it as a black pistol.

8. Investigator McHugh contacted SHERROD, who is the registered owner of the Mercedes. SHERROD admitted to operating the Mercedes, with her husband Eugene Sherrod as a passenger, on the date, time, and at the location of this offense. SHERROD admitted to being involved in the traffic crash and arguing with CW, but she denied ever producing a weapon. SHERROD said that she had a notebook in her hand that was pointed at CW in anger

9. Investigator McHugh contacted the Bureau of Alcohol, Tobacco, Firearms, and Explosives (ATF), the Maryland State Police, and the Maryland Coordination and Analysis Center to conducted firearms registration queries. Neither VASHTI SHERROD, nor her husband Eugene, have registered firearms in Maryland; however, prior to 1996, the state did not require registrations for all firearms.

10. Investigat McHugh contacted members of the Prince George's County Police Department (PGPD), which has jurisdiction in Mitchellville, Maryland, where the Sherrods live. Based on the facts of this case, PG detectives obtained a search warrant for SHERROD's home address, 920 Lake Front Drive, Mitchellville, Maryland.

11. On July 7, 2015, members of the PGPD District 3 Robbery Suppression Team executed the search warrant at S HERROD's home. Investigator McHugh and MPD Detective Sergeant Edelstein were present during the execution of the search warrant. After knocking and announcing the presence of police, SHERROD refused to open the door for police. Detectives attempted to call both SHERROD's cell phone and home phone number to discuss the matter, but she refused to answer. After one hour of attempting to contact and negotiate with SHERROD, PGPD Lieutenant Mrotek ordered that front door of the residence be forced open. Detectives entered the residence and located SHERROD and her husband inside. Detectives then conducted a thorough search of the residence and did not locate any contraband.

12. Based on the facts and circumstances of this offense, it is respectfully requested that an arrest warrant be issued, charging VASHTI ███ SHERROD accordingly.

AFFIANT'S SIGNATURE: [signature]

TO: WARRANT CLERK
PLEASE ISSUE A WARRANT FOR:
Vashti ███ Sherrod

CHARGE WITH: ADW (gun)

Kacu Watson 7/10/15
ASSISTANT UNITED STATES ATTORNEY

SUBSCRIBED AND SWORN BEFORE ME THIS 10th day of July 2015.

[signature]
(JUDGE) (DEPUTY CLERK) SUPERIOR COURT OF THE DISTRICT OF COLUMBIA

Page 3 of 3

CHAPTER 6

Surrender to MPD

My eyes opened, and I glanced over at a window that I did not immediately recognize. It was pitch black, but I could see the US Capitol from the hotel that we checked into the night before. Slowly I became aware of sheets that were not mine and a bed that was not as firm. It was three o'clock in the morning on a day I dreaded like no other day. We were getting dressed for a journey that was not a vacation or a funeral. Even going to a funeral would have been better. I could not feel my body. My lips were trembling. Stunned, shocked, numb that I was facing this in 'the golden years' of my life.

Work was behind me. My children were long grown and gone. I had beautiful grandchildren who were the apple of my eye. My days were filled with cherishing lunch and spa time with my daughter and friends, social events, laughter, and having fun with Gene, who still loved to dance even though he was now visually impaired. Always upbeat, happy, jovial, and loving, my husband was my rock.

We could breathe now and savor all the joys and successes of our lives. We had worked hard to build a successful construction company and janitorial and residential cleaning services. We were blessed to live in Washington, DC, when the city's growing social scene, minority-owned businesses, and civil rights efforts were at their height. Entertaining DC politicians, including mayors, members of the City Council, Superior Court Judges, doctors, and lawyers in our home was not unusual. Attending social events from Presidential Inaugurations and balls to community parties, barbeques, and events with family and friends were some of the joys of our marriage.

Our faith in God was the foundation and glue that held our marriage and family together. Attending church and worshipping together was a top priority in our marriage.

Gene and I were each other's best friends, and we were grateful to wake up together in the morning to a new day the Lord hath made. But never could I have imagined this day.

I was turning my seventy-six-year-old, African American female self into the Fifth District of the Metropolitan Police Department in Southwest DC. A building I had passed a thousand times since the 1960s when my oldest sister Virginia lived in Harbor Square on the waterfront. Yes, the same waterfront in Southwest DC that is now the center of an incredible economic renewal and revival in Washington.

The day was dark and dreary. It was five-thirty in the morning, and no one was moving about except policemen going in and out, out and in. I walked down the sidewalk towards the double wooden doors, and my legs began to shake as I approached the stairs. I squeezed Gene's hand a little tighter, and I could feel Ginger's breath on my neck behind me.

A police officer sat at a mahogany desk at

the entrance. I told him why I was there, and he said, "Have a seat."

On our heels was our pastor, the Reverend Edward James, who arrived at the same time. I looked at the solemn and serious expression on his face. I'd never seen him look that way before. He knew how difficult the day would be for me, my husband, and daughter, Ginger.

My criminal attorney, McDaniel arrived dressed to impress. But he also had a look of sadness that conveyed the gravity of what he knew was coming.

Attorney McDaniel and my pastor had experienced this before, and they both knew I had no idea. We all greeted one another with good morning, and without a word, immediately formed a circle and held hands. My pastor prayed that I would have the strength I needed to get through the day.

A day that I, a perfectionist and planner to a T, did not know what to expect. After praying, my attorney took me aside. He said Detective McHugh would come to get us soon. "Don't say anything," he cautioned, "just let me do the talking."

I said, "Yes, I won't say anything."

We stood there waiting until Detective McHugh came out. "Good morning," he said loudly. "How is everyone today?"

My throat closed up and my eyes focused down to the floor. Both Attorney McDaniel and Gene responded, "Good morning, Detective McHugh." Ginger, my daughter, said nothing. But I could read her as her lips curled up with a slight view of her teeth. This was not a 'good morning' day for her.

"Well, let's go back and look at the video," McHugh said. "Mrs. Sherrod, did you bring your medicine," he asked. I looked at Ginger, and she handed it to me in a neatly folded envelope. It had my morning medications inside—high blood pressure and cholesterol pills. I had to take these at 8:00 a.m. I had already thought to myself no way was I going to take any medication given to me by anyone other than my daughter.

Detective McHugh took the pills and placed

them in his pocket. All I could see was his hands on his waist belt, his intimidating posture, and that substantial black semiautomatic police weapon on his hip. Like the one I supposedly pointed at the woman in front of Gingko's flower shop. It was almost as if he made sure that I saw it. With his sarcastic mantra, "remember me," he already had a way of taunting me. My mind started racing, and all I could think was *I want to live.*

Before I realized it, we were walking to the back of the police station. I had worn my pink two-piece St. John dress and T-strapped shoes thinking I wanted something that would be comfortable and keep me warm for the day. It was early July 2015, and muggy outside, but the court would probably be air-conditioned, and usually, offices were set on low in the summer.

Attorney McDaniel turned and looked at me. "Please come this way," he said.

Detective McHugh led us both into a tiny office with a screen. "I will show you the video that I obtained from in front of the flower shop," he said.

Good, I thought. *Now my lawyer can see what he has been talking about; we can explain it and go home.* To my surprise, the video was concise, and I only saw myself, my car, and my husband in it. My attorney asked a few questions, and then Detective McHugh said he needed to take a mugshot and fingerprint me.

At that moment, the pressure in my body shot up straight to my head. I couldn't say anything because I had promised my attorney that I would not. Detective McHugh led us to the area where they conduct this business. My attorney said, "Mrs. Sherrod, just go through this. Don't say anything, and I will see you later this afternoon."

Later this afternoon, I thought. What? Wait a minute. Where was he going? Surely, he would come back, and we would straighten this out with the judge here.

Detective McHugh called in a female police officer to take my mugshot and fingerprint me. I stayed inside of myself without even breathing loudly. I did not want to make any sudden movement that would indicate I was alive. I felt dead inside. They would not need to kill me, they already had.

I lifted my French manicured fingers into the ink one by one as asked. Pressured each finger down as they rolled them from one side to the next. Finally, I was done. Black ink on my fingers surely would destroy my dress. The female police officer was caring. She looked me in the eyes as if she were confused—lost. I could tell she wanted to know. Why are you here? In that moment, I wished she could tell me why I was there.

There were so many police officers where they sat me. Officers behind desks, coming in for their shift, laughing about their weekends, and guns. Guns everywhere. I hate guns.

Being a country girl, my daddy had shotguns to protect his property. In the corner behind every door in the house, they stood at the ready. We never touched Daddy's guns, but we knew they were there.

I could hear the metal doors opening and closing loudly. The dragging sound of metal touching metal was unbearable. My pressure was off the charts by this point. I felt dizzy and near fainting. The young female officer came and took me to a lock-up cell. She said, "I am about to get off work, and I pray that you are going to be okay."

I began to cry. I could not feel my face. I looked in the holding cell and saw a concrete bench and an open toilet. All I could think was *Vashti, you must stay healthy*. I prayed, and I cried. I asked God, "Why am I being punished like this?"

I could hear Detective McHugh coming. He was making loud noises with the keys and slammed open the door. I thought of my husband and daughter. I needed to survive this moment. Surely it would be over soon. I took a seat, and he dragged the metal doors closed behind me. The sound of those massive weighty doors clinging shut startled me. Tears streamed down my cheeks wetting my face as if I'd been standing outside in the rain.

It was all like a blur. Detective McHugh returned to the cell to give me my medicine. He handed me a glass of water and a folded-up napkin. I assumed it was my medicine, but I most certainly was not going to take it. I politely took the napkin, as he watched, and the water. I gently unfolded it and picked up the medicine and put it in my mouth. What he did not know was that I put it under my tongue. There was no way I would take 'medicine' from him. It could be anything—drugs—to put into my system. As soon as he left, I spat the pills out and flushed them down the toilet.

Time stood still. I felt like I was in a movie that I didn't like. Police officers were in and out. Laughing and talking. Then a police officer came and told me to get up. He presented handcuffs and put them on me.

I did not know that Ginger and Gene were waiting still at the police station entrance, unaware of what was happening to me. Ginger recounts their experience in her own words:

I, Ginger, said to my dad, "I wonder when Mommy is coming out."

"She will be back soon; I am sure, Baby."

My dad still calls me "Baby." I can chuckle

now, but that day I just wanted to scream. I never expected this moment ever. It was surreal. My mother at the po-po. Jail. I watched everything and everyone. Maybe someone would show a glimpse of compassion. There was none, absolutely nothing. Police officers just came and went. I was like, *don't you know who is here? My mother is here right now. Is she okay? Is she going to be okay?* Every cell in my body was on fire. Angry. Scared. Disbelief. Thankfully, our pastor was still with my dad and me. He was trying to be upbeat, but he was getting on my nerves.

"Mr. Sherrod, how long have you and Mrs. Sherrod been married?" our pastor asked.

My dad answered, "Oh, about thirty-five years."

"You must have married her when she was ten." The pastor quipped. Then he and dad chuckled.

I was like, *this is not the time for this banter.* Imagine someone trying to make a bad situation seem lighter, but it was not helping. I looked up and saw Detective McHugh and my mother's attorney.

Attorney McDaniel said, "Mrs. Sherrod will be going to DC Superior Court."

I was in shock. "I thought she was going to see the judge here," I said.

Attorney McDaniel said, "No, she has to go downtown."

I turned to Detective McHugh and asked, "Will you be taking her?"

"Yes," he said.

He lied. I should have known better. But I had no idea that my mother would be going in the Prisoner Transport Van. Booked. Fingerprinted. Mug shot. Handcuffed. *Please wake me up from this nightmare, Lord.*

CHAPTER 7

The Ride

The police van was waiting outback. Detective McHugh took me through a long hallway. Police officers were passing by and laughing, talking about what had happened on their shifts. Absorbing the conversations in detail was not the focus. I was walking to what felt like a black hole in a universe with fear and other emotions warring inside me. Crying was not an option, trying to survive was.

The door swung open and the police van was waiting to whisk me off. My hands were handcuffed in front of me. To say it was comfortable would be a far stretch.

My mind went to how our ancestors must have felt. I was being stripped of my dignity by a man with complete power over me. I had on a pink St. John dress, trimmed in black, but I felt naked. Undignified and clothed in shame, my head was bowed.

Detective McHugh took me to my fate, with no regard for the level of pain or the havoc he was causing a completely innocent woman. A woman with a decent life, past, family, and social standing.

As we approached the police van, a large African American police officer waited. I thought surely he would see that I was a senior citizen, a woman who could be his mother or even grandmother. Surely, he would take care of me, look me in the eyes, and see my pain.

"Get up in the van," he said sternly. The ledge to get up in the van had to be at least a foot from the ground. It was too high for me. The officer got a step stool so that I could get up. But it was still too high for me to get in the van. A steel pole was welded into the second step.

Figuring out how to get up in the van with handcuffs on and T-strapped shoes was a task. At the moment, falling was my greatest fear, but even that paled in comparison to my fear of where I was headed. I raised my foot as high as I could and grabbed the pole in front of me. But I could not pull myself up from the ground. My strength was gone; and even if it were not, I would not have been able to get up in that van.

Before I knew it, another police officer, probably the driver, came around and said loudly, "We have to go, now." Then he put his hands around my arm, and with the other police officer hoisted me up into the van.

The only place to sit was on a long concrete bench on the right or left of the pole. I took my seat. It felt like I should head for the back of the bus where the Negroes were made to sit during the era of Jim Crow South. After all, the van driver was white, and I was black. And race has and will always be a factor in everything. No man other than my husband, son, or doctor has touched my body in forty years. I shivered, trembled, and teared up, feeling dirtier than ever before.

The police van that carried alleged criminals to the lockup horrified me. The concrete bench mounted against the wall on iron poles attached to the ceiling of the truck saved my life. The van driver made so many twists and turns, I stood to hold the pole to keep from falling and to avoid sitting on the concrete bench which aggravated my sciatica back problem. I yelled out, "Please, I am falling."

The husky driver yelled back, "That's why you are here, to be punished."

A young man was also in the van, but he was like a shadow to me. My eyes were glazed in a sea of tears that I willed not to descend down my face for fear that I would break down totally.

In the country, we had horses and donkeys. Riding in the police van felt like I was on a donkey. My body was bumping up and down, my hips and lower back ached. Turns and corners were taken without care for the cargo that was jerked from side to side. To prevent myself from falling, I held on for dear life.

The ride felt like a lifetime, an eternity. I looked out the window as scenes of my life flashed before me. Bouncing through the streets of Washington, I prayed to God. Her spirit was with me telling me to be strong. Daddy was holding me up and I could hear him say, "Know who you are, baby girl."

We were told Daddy named all his children, but I believe my mother named me. What father would name his daughter 'Vashti' from the Book of Esther in the Bible? Vashti, a woman who defied her husband King Ahasuerus' request to come before him wearing her royal crown and display her beauty to his guests. Angry at her refusal, her husband decided to punish her indolence because it might incite the wives of Persia to disobey their husbands. Vashti was replaced by Esther as the king's wife, and a dictate went throughout the land that all husbands dominate their households. My mother's message through my name was: I am a queen. I am powerful. I am independent. I am beautiful. Thank you, Mother, for that blessing. I needed it that day more than any other day in my life. But I was breaking, losing myself today. I don't know if I will every reclaim me again.

The police van stopped, and I assumed we had arrived at the courthouse. It was dark so I figured we were underground in a parking lot below the building. From the window, I saw new faces, more police officers and guards. The doors swung open and a police officer stood there telling me to come out. I stood up carefully, my legs felt like logs and my back ached from the harrowing journey across DC's pothole laden streets. Grabbing the pole, I decided to slide down using my hands instead of stepping at least the one foot down from the top step. I landed safely, and the police officer guided me to an open door.

All I could think was *Lord, please help me.* Like one of my childhood ponies on our farm, the fear inside my heart raced with abandon, wild and free.

My father built our colonial home on a hill on his own land. My paternal grandparents lived with us until they died. My grandfather, Sam Sanders, a freed slave and cook in the Union Army was listed as being 100 years old on the 1940 census. My grandmother, Watsie

Sanders was also a freed slave. She was a homemaker and helped my mother raise ten children. Both of my grandparents were born in South Carolina with Catawba Indian heritage. Daddy always said their motto was "only the strong survive." As I endured the procedure of being processed in at the jail, their motto held me up.

At the jail, I was instructed to obey all orders. If not, "things could get ugly." I could not stop crying. I was in handcuffs and ankle chains.

To take my mind off the ordeal, I thought about the time I won a statewide-oratorical contest at ten years old. My sister Virginia, who was living in Washington, DC, sent me a new dress and a new pair of shoes. She wanted me to look extra special for that night when people from all over the state of South Carolina came to together for the contest.

My daddy and our entire family attended. He was so proud of his 'baby girl' because I won the contest. The prize included a trophy and cash. I recited my favorite poem from memory, a poem that meant a lot to me as a young woman. Other than the Holy Bible, this poem helped me be a proud young Black girl growing up in the Jim Crow South, and to always believe in Myself.

MYSELF

I have to live with myself and so
I want to be fit for myself to know.
I want to be able as days go by,
always to look myself straight in the eye;
I don't want to stand with the setting sun
and hate myself for the things I have done.
I don't want to keep on a closet shelf
a lot of secrets about myself
and fool myself as I come and go
into thinking no one else will ever know
the kind of person I really am,
I don't want to dress up myself in sham.
I want to go out with my head erect
I want to deserve all men's respect;
but here in the struggle for fame and wealth
I want to be able to like myself.
I don't want to look at myself and know that
I am bluster and bluff and empty show.
I never can hide myself from me;
I see what others may never see;
I know what others may never know,

I never can fool myself and so,
whatever happens I want to be
self-respecting and conscience free.
Edward Albert Guest

CHAPTER 8

Incarcerated

Still in handcuffs, I was escorted to the back of the courthouse, and they gave me a number.

A man at the gate asked me, "What are you in here for?"

I said, "I am being locked up."

He said, "I know that, but why?"

I said, "For nothing."

He said, "They are all lined up ready to go in."

The men were Black men, young mostly, some older with graying hair. Orange jumpsuits. Orange is not the new black. It has always been black. I felt like I was watching a television show, and then thrown onto the set as one of the actors.

They led me in through a door, down a hallway. I felt a million eyes on me. There were a few women, but I was the oldest one. As I went down the hall, there were cells with men locked up. Men, staring at me. The long hallway felt like the door of no return that slaves passed through before getting on the boat to the Americas from Africa.

Having worked at the Smithsonian early in my career, I was well versed in African American history – particularly the slave trade. Working in the Smithsonian Castle, Arts and Industries, Division of the Performing Arts, and the Anacostia Neighborhood Museum provided me with unique insights into our culture. The museum's director and my boss, John Kinard frequently traveled to Africa, particularly Ghana. Photos of the Door of No Return at the Cape Coast slave castle built by the Swedes were part of exhibits at the Museum in Southeast Washington.

At the end of the hall lined with jail cells, an African American woman in a uniform was waiting for me. She put me in a jail cell by myself and said, "Sit in here and wait. I'll be back with a bucket that you can pee in." There were women in other small cells around me.

Eventually, she came with a cup, and I peed in it. They moved me from the cell, and I headed down the hall.

I knew she was an employee there, but I wasn't sure what she did. "Come down here," she said. "I am going to search you."

I obeyed and came closer. She uncuffed me for the first time in what seemed like hours. To my shock and horror, she said, "Remove your top and your bra."

Apparently, my delay and the look on my face angered her. "Take it off," she snarled. "I don't have all day."

I disrobed, taking off my jacket and setting it down on a bench. My dress was a black sheath with a long zipper down the back. I struggled to get it unzipped; finally, it came down low enough to take it below my shoulders.

"Take it all the way off," she bellowed while looking at me, examining me as my dress fell to the floor.

I stepped out of it and just left it there.

"Take off your bra! Can you hear?"

I unhooked my bra and placed it on my

jacket. Her hands immediately began touching my breasts, going underneath them, cupping them.

"Raise your arms!"

I obeyed.

"Girl, how old are you? You are as old as I am! You must have done something terrible to get in here. This is what you get."

I stopped breathing, I think, at least down to a whisper.

"How old are you?" she asked again.

I did not answer her.

"You are at least sixty. Your girls appear to be sixty years old," she said, laughing at me. "Stop crying," she demanded. "I will not feel sorry for your dressed up old ass. You should not have did what you did."

My body was shaking uncontrollably. I started thinking about when I was a little girl in South Carolina, and a woman's body was found under the school building. We could see her body. Her clothes had been removed, she only had on her panties. As a southern child, it was a horror that she had been killed.

We did not understand rape, but that is what happened to her. In the south, at that time, the police did not conduct a formal investigation. That body was left there as a message to us kids. This is what will happen to you if you step the wrong way. To this day, we never learned who killed that woman, who she was, or why she died.

I was being stripped searched. But I would survive this. As long as my body was not found under a bridge or a building, I would survive this. *God, help me. I am Vashti, your child, the daughter of Cazetta and Marion Sanders. This woman will not destroy me, even though she is trying to crush my spirit with her cruelty.*

"Take off your panties," she said gruffly.

I took a deep breath and complied. She took her hand and probed between my legs and my backside, laughing the entire time. She removed her gloves and threw them in the trash can. "Take off your shoes!"

I had to sit down to unbuckle my T-straps. Since I no longer had on underwear, I sat on my dress so my skin would not touch the bench. I removed my shoes and handed them to her. She examined them inside and out and looked at the bottom. After she was done, she threw my shoes as far as she could down the hall. "You can get dressed now."

I did not know this woman's name, but I shall never forget her as long as I live. Her cruel, evil nature will come back to haunt her. Doing a job well can be respected no matter what it is. She had a job to do, but she chose to do it with cruelty. As she stood in front of me, I wanted to hit her with those chains. She re-shackled my hands, but they were in reach of her throat. I could only fantasize about it. I would not do it if I could. I had never hit anyone in my life, outside of my brother Ronnie Shay and my own children, whom I lightly spanked.

"Go get your shoes and go to the end of the hall to your cellblock!" my handler yelled. "Can you hear?" she said again. "Take your old ass down the hall!"

I picked up my shoes with my still handcuffed hands and chains around my ankle and headed down the hall where another woman waited.

The woman took my arm and guided me around the corner. There were people everywhere: men, women— almost 100% black. As I passed by the cells, inmates were standing, sitting, lying down on the floor, and using the toilet where all could see. There were no chairs. With my eyes downcast towards the floor, I tried not to look.

There were some memories I did not want to stay in my spirit. I was overflowing with stress, sadness, and memories that would never leave me. I prayed to God that I could laugh one day. He said that He would never leave me or forsake me, and that He would never give me more than I could bear. But this burden felt too heavy for me, and the yoke was not easy.

Barely able to walk, I was escorted down a long hall. Ladies were peering through the open iron bars that enclosed the cells, cursing and yelling as I passed by. I was scared to death. I was initially locked up in a cell alone, then moved to the general population which was filled with young women of color sitting against walls or lying on the concrete with their hands under their heads.

CHAPTER 9

Grandma, Why Are You Here?

We arrived at the cell where I would be placed for a time unknown to me. The lady unlocked the metal doors and opened them for me to go in. I started crying. This was it. This was the reason I was here. The ultimate punishment.

Jail. For something that I was completely innocent of. *Lord, shore me up. Lord, hold my hand. Lead me on, let me stand. I am tired. I am weary. I am worn. Through this storm, through this night, take my hand, precious Lord, and lead me on.* I could only think to sustain myself through the Holy word. I remembered that Shadrach, Meshach, and Abednego from the Book of Daniel survived the fiery furnace by keeping their faith in God. The fire had no power over their bodies, nor was a hair on their head singed, neither was their coats changed or the smell of fire on them when they emerged from the furnace.

I opened my eyes to ten young Black women. Some were standing, some leaning on the walls, some sitting on the floor with their heads back, some were laying down on the floor asleep. Most of the women just looked at me, making eye contact with me through my tears. I looked around to see if there was a chair. There was no place to sit, so, I found an unoccupied corner and used the wall to help me slide down to the floor. I sat there for what felt like an eternity.

A couple of the women chattered among themselves as they looked at me. One, whose name I later learned as "Shawn" asked me, "Grandma, why are you in here? You in jail all dressed up. Don't you know you going to be sitting on the floor all day till you get out of here?"

I could not process her question.

Someone else said, "Umm, she probably never been in here before, Shawn. Leave her alone."

I started crying harder.

Shawn said, "Girl, stop crying, you are making me messed up. It ain't going to help you get out of here. Maybe you thought that dress would, but you in here now so get it together. We can't stand all that cryin'."

I heard them and realized, yes, I better get it together because I might be in here for a long time. I wiped my tears with my hands, flicked my hair up, and then took in my surroundings.

Most of the women were probably in their twenties. Some were attractive, had their nails done; some were not. It occurred to me that some may be in here for serious crimes, and others for almost nothing. I learned the latter as they shared their stories with me.

Shawn asked again, "Grandma, what are you in here for? What did you do? You don't seem like you could have done anything to be in jail. Did you have a fight with your man?"

The women laughed. "I bet she tore him up," another woman said. "Old ladies know how to tear-up some ass, and not eeeee—ven leave a mark. Just ask my grandmother. She would take out that switch and tear us up and not leave a welp. But with a man, hot grits were the tool of choice. It would burn and turn their skin raw and make them pay for what they did."

"I know. I am in here because of a man."

"Shit."

"That MF had the nerve to call the police on me twice. The next time they came, they just took me in."

"That's why I am here now. I have been here for three days. I don't even know where my kids are. I can't call my job. I only got one phone call and that was to my friend, who I asked to go check on my kids. I can't sleep, can't eat, because I don't know where my children are."

As I listened to each woman go through their story, my heart sank. Here I was worried about me and what had happened to me. I had the right to be worried, but these women did not know where their kids were. Most of them were in here because of a fight with a boyfriend, a family member, or some other minor infraction.

"We have all told you what we are in here for, Grandma, and you still haven't told us why you are here," Shawn said again.

"Oh, leave her alone, Shawn, she doesn't want to talk to us."

"She got it like that."

"Probably from some high-falutin family, bougie, bullshit and a man with fine crinkly hair and buttercream skin."

Laughter permeated the cell. Some went around the room and slapped hands and did a snap thing.

My daughter does the bump, but I refuse to do that. I do not see the purpose. She and her husband have a special bump that seems to go on for five minutes and ends with them flicking their fingers on each other's hands. Dumb. Just dumb.

But I must admit if it were not for their conversation, I would still be crying. They were quite humorous.

"Grandma, how much did that dress cost?"

"And those shoes, they look like cobbie cuddlers."

"Something I saw my teachers wearing in school."

"That cute little strap that cross over the foot and back the other way."

"T-straps," I said.

"Oh, now she talks."

"Okay, Grandma, you have something to say."

"Yes, the shoes are referred to as T-straps."

Everyone laughed. "Oh, for real?" another woman said. "I will remember those T-straps like a T-bone steak."

More laughter permeated the cell.

"Well, where did you get them, and why are you dressed up like this?"

"You didn't know you were coming to jail today?"

I said, "no."

"Well, where did you think you were going?"

"I thought I was going to see the judge," I said.

"Um, um, um," a woman who was lying on the floor with her back turned to us said. She rolled over to face us. She was about six months pregnant; her eyes were red, and her arms bruised.

"What the F are y'all doing? Leave her alone. She ain't used to all of this mess. Don't you see she's old and could die being in here? We are used to this shit. She ain't. Cut her some slack."

The room quieted under her rebuke. It felt good to be cared for, for a change. Since I'd left my family and my attorney, this young lady was the first person to show me empathy.

As I listened to each of them, I started to feel a little less stressed. At least I was not in a cell alone.

A female bailiff came to the door and motioned me over. I got up off the floor, which took some time, and walked slowly over to her. My back was really, really hurting now, and my legs and ankles were swollen. As I neared her, I saw a little stool and a wall with an opening in it. I sat down on the stool, happy to be sitting on a chair. I peered over the wall and there was my attorney! I was so glad to see him, I wept.

"I told you I would see you as soon as I could," he said.

I continued to weep.

"Vash, it is your turn to bless the food." My daddy had each of us say a blessing at dinner time. It was not just "God is great, God is good, and we thank him for our food." It was a real blessing. The requirement was to say a verse or scripture from the Bible. It had to be correct and verbatim. Daddy would say the closing prayer, and then we would eat. My stepmother was a wonderful Christian woman. She called my daddy, "Mr. Sanders" in front of us kids.

My stepmother served us the food she made for dinner that evening, but dinner was at lunch time because everyone was so hungry. Fried chicken, gravy, mashed potatoes, greens, homemade rolls, and iced tea were spread across our big round mahogany table. The table, big enough to seat at least fifteen people, was set with china, a linen tablecloth and napkins. This is how we ate every day.

I offered my prayer, which was "Jesus wept." Usually, this small prayer made Daddy mad, but he did not say anything this time.

I looked at my attorney and thought, *Jesus wept*. Knowing that my Savior was persecuted, tried and died for something he did not do calmed me. I thought of Jesus standing before the crowd as they screamed, "Crucify Him, crucify Him."

Surely, I could get through this. I looked up at my attorney and tried to smile. "I am so glad to see you," I said.

He looked at me with big brown eyes that seemed to touch my soul and said, "How are you doing, Mrs. Sherrod?"

I said, "I am holding on."

"Good," he responded. "I have worked everything out. It is going to be okay."

I had no idea what he was talking about, but I listened intently.

He said, "I have a friend who works here. We went to school together, and she is going to see you. I explained the situation to her, and she is going to help."

As I processed his statement, it appeared to me that he was saying something without saying it. I understood. As a businesswoman and wise almost eighty-year-old, I knew sadly that justice was bought, even though it was paid with a price.

My attorney was expensive. So, this was how it worked. My first experience at what I have seen most of my life. White people get criminal charges every day. They are often much more egregious than any charge of the women that I was with in the cellblock.

With the means to buy justice, you get a slap on the wrist. No losing your employment or worrying about where your children were. It was all taken care of, neatly, cleanly, like wrapping a Christmas present. Edges pressed and taped down so the jagged cuts cannot be seen. The ribbon pulled tightly around the box and smoothed out so there were no bumps or crinkles and tied up nicely in a bow with each loop the same perfect size, exploding like a bouquet of flowers.

Yes, people with means never are accountable when they need to avoid paying the price for what they did. In my case, I was innocent and a woman with means.

The girls in my cellblock? They might have been innocent or guilty, but one thing they were not was women with means.

"Well, thank you, Attorney McDaniel."

"You are welcome," he said. "I will see you again a bit later, just hold on and be patient."

I nodded my head and gave him a slight smile.

I ended up back in the same cell block after talking to my attorney. However, this time, I had hope that maybe this would have a positive outcome.

Why did the Lord put me in this position? I asked myself. In church, my favorite hymns were "Precious Lord" and "If I Can Help Somebody." Blessing someone else can take away the pain so I went back to that cellblock not as an inmate, but as a Christian woman, strong and mighty; a woman blessed with years, wisdom and knowledge, and one who might be able to impact the life of one of these women that my journey had intersected with.

I walked back in, slid down the wall until my buttocks hit the hard, cold, cement floor. "Did I miss anything?" I asked.

No one responded, so I asked louder, "Did I miss anything?"

That got their attention. Shawn said, "No, Grandma, you didn't miss anything. Where did you go?"

I said, "I went to speak with my attorney."

The pregnant woman lying on the floor sat up. "I've been here for four days," she said, "and I haven't seen a lawyer. They said I would be seeing one soon, but nothin'."

"What are you in here for?" I asked her.

She said, "Drug possession. I had just bought me some, and I got caught."

"But you are pregnant," I said.

"Really, Grandma. You never seen a pregnant junkie? You still haven't told us why you are here."

At that moment, I had their captive attention and wanted to share. The women, in however they found themselves that day, were all looking at me. Dying to know my story. A story that I had not even told my children. The shame of it. But why? I had not done anything. I was the same mother, wife, daughter, woman. *Why the shame?* I thought. Free yourself, Vashti. Unshackle your mind and let it go.

I told them my story. I knew it by heart by now. "My husband and I were parked—"

"I told y'all that it had something to do with a man," Shawn said.

"I bet she cut him after he told her he met a younger woman and wanted a divorce!"

They laughed out loud. "Yeah girl," the woman who was on the floor and pregnant stood up. "You go, sistah, you might look like a church mom, but you ain't no different than a mad black woman!"

"No," I said. "it wasn't that. We were at the flower shop to purchase flowers for our yard."

"Oh wow, now that is a good one. You and your hubby were out there shopping for flowers?"

"Aww, how cute."

"Is your husband Black?"

"Yes, he is," I said.

They stared at me until Shawn broke the awkward silence. "He's a Black man and he was with you buying flowers? Now that is a real man."

"A man who goes with his wife on stuff like that... I ain't never heard of that."

"Tell us more, Grandma."

I picked up my story. "Shortly after we got there, a woman tried to park her truck in the space behind our car. She hit the left side mirror of our car. When she pulled forward, she hit it again. I tried to get her attention by yelling, 'stop, stop.' She continued to back up, hitting my mirror. She realized it, stopped, and then left her vehicle. I, too, got out of my car to examine the damage to the mirror. The woman said, 'Push the mirror back; I can push my mirror to move them in place.' I told her my mirrors were electronic. She said, 'you need a better car.' She was cursing at this point, using the "F-word" as she talked. Then she said, 'Let's exchange insurance information since the police will take too long.' I agreed. My husband disagreed and told me to call the police. She went to cursing at us again, continuing to use the F- word. She said that her dog had just died, and husband had left her for another woman. She repeated, 'I don't f-ing need this.'

"We went to exchange insurance information except she had no insurance card or up to date registration. The lady called her insurance company and requested that they email her the information on her insurance card. I copied it on my pad from her phone. She copied my insurance information from my insurance card. I finally said in a gentle tone, 'I can see why he left you.' She then replied, 'he did not leave me for a Black nigger woman like you. He likes white women.' Then she opened her front passenger door too wide hitting the front left fender of our car. I walked near the rear of my car's left fender to see whether she touched the back of our vehicle while backing up. I also looked at her rear side bumper next to us but saw no damage. She continued to curse at me saying, 'you keep your F-ing car in a garage.' Then she drove off driving fast, too fast to be on a city street. Her insurance, USAA paid for all damage that she caused."

Somehow, I managed to get it all out. I finally told my cellmates what happened. I didn't look up to see their faces while I was talking, I just kept going and going until I got to the end. Or at least what I thought was the end.

The unscrupulous power of an out of control, racist, bigoted, despicable police officer was the only apparent reason why he would do this to two senior citizens. Tears rolled down my face, and I felt exhausted and quite ill. I hadn't eaten all day.

Shawn noticed that I didn't look well and called out to one of the guards. "Hey, hey," she said in a loud voice. "We need help here. She is sick! Grandma is sick! Hey, help her!"

"Maybe I should ask to be taken to the hospital," I said.

"Oh no, girl, don't do that," Shawn said. "You will be in the hospital under lockup, and after you get better, they will bring you right back here and start you all over again. That will be a setback."

Oh, no, I thought. *I can't have any other setbacks.* I wouldn't make it.

A white female appeared at the door to our cell. She peered in, and Shawn pointed at me.

The lady unlocked the doors and stepped in. "Are you okay?" she asked.

"No, I don't feel well." I started to cry. I couldn't believe I had more tears.

"Get up and come with me," she said.

I struggled to get up, as my hands were still cuffed. I had no idea what was going to happen next, but the door was open, and I walked through it. I felt the eyes of everyone in the cell on me. This was it; we were parting to never see each other again. As I slid past them, I could hear some sniffling. I believe someone was crying.

"Goodbye, Grandma," I heard. "We are so sorry this happened to you. It was just plain wrong."

Shawn said, "Well, we will see you on the

news after taking the damn police department down."

"Yeah, yeah, you make sure you get them, bastards."

"Just remember us. Remember what you saw in here. We are in here with nothing and nowhere to go, and no one to help us."

"Take care, Grandma," said another.

Finally, I turned and looked at them, trying to take it all in. "Goodbye, ladies, take care," I told them.

Then I walked out, and the guard closed the door.

CHAPTER 10

SAVING GRACE

"Where am I going now?" I asked.

"I am taking you to a cell with a concrete bench to sit down and a private toilet."

The guard led me down the hall, and once again, I passed by men and women in lockup. We stopped, and she opened the doors to a tiny cell. It was about five by five, like the half bath in my foyer. I was glad to see I would be alone. I guessed this was a step up for me. I fell on the concrete bench, which was hard, but at least I was not on the floor. I was so weak and dizzy I just leaned my head on my hands.

"I will bring you some lunch," the guard said.

She was a white female with blond hair and blue eyes. She stood out like a fly in buttermilk. *An unusual career* was my first thought about her. She was incredibly soft in appearance, but probably tough as nails. I was thankful for the compassion she offered me.

"Here you go," she said. "It's a bologna sandwich. Would you like some coffee?"

"No, thank you," I said. There wasn't a sink to wash my hands, which caused anxiety because of the filth around me.

She handed the sandwich to me, and I realized it was white bread with no mayo or mustard. We only ate fried bologna sandwiches. I peeled off the bread and looked inside. I was starving. It looked safe to eat, so I took a small bite.

This cell was certainly better than the one before. I could still hear the banging of cell doors, loud voices, yelling and cursing. I didn't know what was next, but I thanked God for a concrete bench.

After some time, I heard footsteps and rattling chains approaching my cell. I looked up and saw a female guard holding chains. She opened the door to my cell and stepped in. "It's time to see the judge," she said.

Great, I thought. I stood up to go, but before

I knew it, she took my arms and placed heavy iron shackles on my wrist, around my waist, leading down to my feet. My feet were chained together, and my hands were connected to the chain around my waist. I was numb, sickened by the thought of my body being in shackles. *Like how our ancestors who were shackled and placed on boats heading to America,* I thought.

My feet moved slowly, pulling the weight with my legs, lower back, and shoulders. It really hurt, and I was following her slowly. Faint and weak, I fell a couple of times and struggled to get back up.

The guard asked, "Why are you here? Why are you in here?"

I told her I was charged with an ADW – Assault with a Deadly Weapon – but hadn't done anything and there was a video to prove it.

"You are innocent until proven guilty," she said. "I hope this is the case because I am concerned about your survival at your age."

We returned to the same hall where everyone was looking from behind their bars. I slid past the cell holding my 'grandchildren,' the ladies I met in our shared cell, and as I passed by, every one of them stood up and began to wave.

"Take care, Grandma!"

"Good luck, Grandma!"

Tears welled up in my eyes as I thought about my own grandchildren. I thanked God that they would never see me in this manner.

I was filled with anger, so much anger that I wished I could break those chains and... *How dare they do this to me!*

I passed many cells before I reached the end of the hall to join a group of inmates all in chains! The directional signs indicated the doors to the courtroom. The judge was around the corner. There were four other inmates with me, two men and two women. We were all lined up, and as we stepped toward the door, the guard instructed us to not look at anyone, turn our heads, or look at any individual in the courtroom. "Look straight ahead and don't move around in your chairs," she said.

Waiting to go into the courtroom, I read the sign above my head. Do *not turn your heads and look at the courtroom.* We were led into the courtroom and directed to an enclosed box with glass around it. We took our seats, and one by one was presented to the judge when she called our name.

I struggled to get up and move along with the guard towards the front of the courtroom. I did not look at anyone as instructed, but I did see my Attorney Brian McDaniel. I was feeling better at this point because he was there with me.

I turned to face the judge, and she said in a loud booming voice, "Good afternoon, Mrs. Sherrod." She was African American with long hair, beautiful skin, and white teeth. Her smile was warm and radiant. She made me feel so much better, like there was someone who understood that I did not belong here.

I delightfully returned the greeting, "Good afternoon, your honor."

As soon as I got the greeting out, she proceeded to talk to the prosecution. She had several pages of papers in her hands and began to flip through them. "What are the charges here? I see some pages missing that should be here," the judge said to the prosecution.

"Your honor let me see; I don't have any additional papers," responded the prosecution. The female DC government lawyer was quite unorganized in her appearance and demeanor. I could not believe this was happening. She could not even state the charges.

"Your honor, my client is being charged with assault with a deadly weapon," responded Attorney McDaniel. "These charges were made by the claimant, but there is a videotape that does not show a gun. The police officer who submitted the charging documents stated that the videotape shows my client walking towards the claimant with arms stretched pointing a gun similar to a police officer's semiautomatic weapon."

"Is that your understanding?" she asked the prosecution.

The prosecution responded, "I believe so. We will determine—"

"That is enough," responded the judge. She lifted the gavel and banged it lightly on her desk. The judge turned towards me and looked me in the eyes. "Mrs. Sherrod, I am releasing you today on your own recognizance. I ask that you not come within 500 feet of the claimant and obey all the District of Columbia laws."

I responded, "I will, your Honor."

She again lifted her gavel, and as she pounded her desk said, "Next case."

Before I knew it, the guard approached, unlocked the handcuffs on my wrists, and removed the shackles around my waist and ankles. I stepped out of them, and Attorney McDaniel quickly walked toward me, grabbed my hand, and assisted me out of the front of the courtroom. I was limp and could barely walk. I felt so weak from the day's journey.

As soon as we approached the wooden gate to walk through the people sitting in the courtroom, I immediately saw my family. Gene, Ginger, and Pastor James were coming toward me. I fell into Gene's arm, and both he and Ginger wrapped their arms around me. They were crying, and I began to cry too. Pastor James also hugged me. It was like a family reunion. We practically walked out of the courtroom holding each other.

Attorney McDaniel held the huge mahogany doors open, and we found ourselves in the hallway. He informed me that I was free to go home and he would call me the following day to discuss the next steps.

I really couldn't process it at all. Walking through the throngs of people in the DC Superior Court felt surreal. I still felt like I was in shackles and in jail. I could not stop crying. I knew I looked awful. Everyone had to be looking at us. When we finally reached the front door, it was the first time I had had fresh air since six o'clock that morning. The sun was up, and everything around me business as usual. But it was not for me.

I had been locked up in jail and imprisoned. My shoulders were slumped, and it still felt like Gene was holding me up to keep me from collapsing on the ground.

Attorney McDaniel looked at me one final time and said, "Mrs. Sherrod, you are going to be okay. I will make sure of that."

All I could muster was, "Thank you, I hope so."

He told everyone goodnight, and Gene, Ginger, and Pastor James said their goodbyes to him. My pastor had driven Gene and Ginger to DC Superior Court early that morning to meet me, which meant we could get back to the hotel quickly to pick up our car. Before I knew it, his car was in front of ours, and Gene and Ginger helped me get in the car.

No one said a word. We were happy the day was over and praising God that the judge let me go on my own recognizance. We did not have time to pray, but I knew that we would do that later.

We pulled away from DC Superior Court and turned down Indiana Avenue, making a right turn in front of the Metropolitan Police Department headquarters. There were lots of police cars parked along the street, and I began to shiver.

Gene was holding my hand and must have felt me shaking. "Are you okay, Vash?" he asked.

"Yes, I'm okay," I said. "I'm just having a moment."

We made a left onto Constitution Avenue, and I looked straight up at the Capitol. At that moment, my heart sank thinking about what the Constitution meant. Constitutional rights meant too much to me. Both Gene and I had participated in the civil rights marches and movements; me, in South Carolina, and eventually in Washington, DC, where I moved to achieve my educational goals.

As far as I was concerned, my hard-fought civil rights had been shredded and walked over. I was charged, booked, handcuffed, searched, shackled, and imprisoned because a woman told an obvious lie. There was a video. There was an eyewitness. I had no criminal record, no unpaid parking tickets, no registered gun, no gun at all—ever. Still, I found my seventy-seven-year-old self in jail.

CHAPTER 11

Home, But Not Free

By August, I felt better than I had in a long time. A long time from May 15th – the day I went to jail. I was still struggling with triggers, but my depression had lifted somewhat. The day was filled with hope.

My head was higher, and I walked with more strength and security. Gene even got a smile out of me with all my white teeth showing. I had worked a long time to have a beautiful smile. Many people my age have bad teeth. But I felt it was essential for me to look my best, especially this particular day.

We were, once again, at the Hyatt Regency on Capitol Hill. The pre-trial hearing was today at D.C. Superior Court. I had not been back since being locked up in jail. I had never been associated with a pre-trial hearing, which made me anxious. But I also felt empowered because I would get a chance to tell my story. Now the ball was in my court.

Attorney McDaniel would share the evidence that I did not have a gun and did not physically threaten the claimant. On the video, she clearly appeared to be the aggressor. All the judge had to do was look at the video... at least that's what I thought.

Gene and I laughed together in a way that we had not in months. Ginger was at the hotel with us coordinating everything. The phone in our hotel room rang, and it was her. "Mommy, are you ready to go?"

"Yes, we are pretty much all set."

"Well, how are you doing," she asked.

"I feel like everything is going to be okay. I just can't wait until this is all over."

Ginger said, "It will be over today, and we will go celebrate tonight. I'm just thankful the nightmare will be over today. I'm on my way downstairs and will stop by your room."

"Okay, do you think it will be easy to get a cab?"

"Yes, Mommy. They are all lined up out

front like people trying to get into a Prince concert."

As soon as I (Ginger) rose my hand to knock on my parents' hotel door, it swung open and out stepped my mother looking like a vogue model. "Wow, you look beautiful, Mommy."

"Thanks, Ginger," she said. "I am ready. I feel like a free woman today."

"Good, I know that is true and that our prayers will be answered."

My daughter looked gorgeous, and I was so proud of her. Ginger was wearing a darker green suit trimmed in black. I believe it was a Misook, which is a lighter version of St. John. She wore black pumps and carried a matching green leather purchase. Coincidentally, her outfit complemented what Gene and I had selected to wear for the court appearance.

Gene, arrayed in a mint green silk tie with matching handkerchief, looked dapper as always. I had chosen my light green St. John suit trimmed in vanilla silk with crystal buttons, and I agreed with Ginger that I looked great. My crystal necklace and earrings accentuated the buttons in a graceful manner.

My shoes were Ferragamo crème, and my purse was a Chanel crème quilted jumbo shoulder bag. I wanted to look my best for the judge. Like a woman of stature who would never own a semiautomatic weapon and point it at anyone in a menacing manner – the look of success, class.

This ADW charge was clearly vengeance from an angry white woman with mental health concerns and a white police officer who believed her. Perhaps they were friends or dating. Perhaps he thought Gene and I mocked his power.

Who knew what really happened to bring me to this day? At least it felt like the fog was beginning to lift. Anticipating our appearance at Superior Court for my pre-trial before Judge Sullivan, I could finally see some distance in front of me.

Our hotel was close, so we had a short ride in an air-conditioned taxi. The cab driver pulled in front and wished us a good day.

Gene, who was sitting up front, said: "Yes, it will be a good day. Thank you."

It was sweltering, like being in a sauna with the sun as the lamp. Steamrolled from the streets, and people talked in whispers because it was too hot to speak. Letting the warm air into your mouth and lungs just made you hotter.

Everyone in front of the courthouse looked hot and sweaty, perspiring as if they had been running track. The walk from the curbside to the front door was approximately 100 feet, long enough for the heat of the day to warm our skin.

Going through the security check to enter Superior Court and seeing those big burly security guards with large guns on their hips staring at us made my neck tight. They were probably as afraid of me as I was of them, on alert for potential danger not knowing who might pull a gun on them.

Sure. A little old lady in a mint green St. John dress. Ridiculous, I thought.

In that small amount of time, I had created

more drama in my overactive, anxious mind than I actually experienced going through the security process. The security guards were nothing but kind. "Mam, please put your purse in this basket. If you could step forward, I will wand you. Now please turn around."

I followed each command, knowing that I wanted to do as they stated. I have respect for the police and anyone in security whose job is to protect us. I doubted any of these men would ever believe I was here to present myself before a judge in Superior Court to face charges of assault with a deadly weapon.

Gene, Ginger, and I walked quite a distance before we found the courtroom I was scheduled to appear in. Along the way, I observed the men and women who found themselves in court this day. They were mostly young African Americans, primarily men and women with children. The attorneys, dressed in dark suits and white shirts or blouses, were evident. Most had briefcases and had an air of sophistication, almost arrogance.

The rest of us had a look in our eyes like

we did not know what would happen next. What situation brought these people to Superior Court on this day? Had anyone else been falsely accused like me? Perhaps they faced parking violations, child support, divorce, or criminal charges like me. No one liked going before a judge, but all one could do was pray and hope for the best.

At least that's what I was doing, praying and hoping for the best. I did not know why I was so nervous. I knew my attorney would do a good job, and I believed that once the judge saw the videotape, he would throw out the case.

I tried to remain patient and not become overly frustrated as we searched for the courtroom. My blood pressure was already elevated. I could feel it coursing through my veins.

"Here it is, Mommy," Ginger said. "It is on this floor."

As we approached Courtroom 42, I could see a well-dressed woman sitting on a light tan bench watching us. She wore a lovely yellow suit and a beautifully coifed haircut; her legs were crossed at the ankles. Something looked familiar about her, but I was still too far away. As we approached, she stood. She had lovely-shaped legs, almost like a dancer. Moving gracefully, with a rod straight back, she turned towards us. As we neared, my heart smiled. It was Reverend Burnett, a minister from Alfred Street Baptist Church. I could not believe that she was here to support me.

I had never interacted with the reverend over the years, yet God blessed me with one of his shepherds. She held her arms out towards me. I embraced her, feeling refreshed from the loveliness of her perfume. "Good morning, Mrs. Sherrod," she said warmly.

Tears welled in my eyes. "Good morning, Reverend Burnett."

"Call me Donna," she said. "We are family."

"I am so glad to see you, Donna." We linked hands and sat together. Ginger and Gene joined us on the bench too.

"You look wonderful, Mrs. Sherrod." I did not know what to say. I did not feel beautiful, but I did feel better knowing she was there.

"Well, it is a hard day for me. I do not know what to expect, but as soon as the judge sees the video, it will all be over. I know you don't know what I am charged with, but I will tell you briefly."

Her deep brown eyes looked at mine, and I could feel her spirit. I shared with her what I was accused of and that I was innocent. "There is a video that proves it, as well as an eyewitness."

"Just awful," she said, "and how terrible for this to happen to you and your family. We all know what this is about. It is a shame this type of blatant racism is still going on."

I nodded in agreement.

About that time, my lawyer Attorney McDaniel appeared. I could not help but notice that he had on a tan windowpane suit. The pant legs were flared, and the lapel was too large. I am sure it was expensive, but it was not becoming.

"Good morning, Mrs. Sherrod, Mr. Sherrod," he said. "I had a chance to look at the video, the full video, and plan to show it to the judge today."

"Great, I exclaimed!" This was good news. The nightmare would soon be over. "Let's head into the courtroom, Mrs. Sherrod," he said.

"Wait, let us pray before going in," said Reverend Burnett.

"Oh, I am so sorry, I did not introduce you. Attorney McDaniel, this is Reverend Burnett from our church."

Each greeted the other with 'nice to meet you' as we proceeded to form a small circle to pray. "Father, we thank you for today, another day that you hath made. We know that you will take care of us and not let any harm come to us. Lord, we ask that you strengthen Vashti as she seeks justice. You are the God of justice and will have the final say in all things. We ask this in the name of your son Jesus Christ. Amen." Everyone said 'amen' and squeezed hands.

The prayer gave me a renewed sense of strength and empowerment. As I walked into the courtroom, I remembered my daddy always saying, “No weapon formed against you shall prosper.”

I found a seat where Gene, Ginger, Reverend Burnett, and I could all sit together. Attorney McDaniel headed up to the judge’s bench, where he sat at the table on the left. The judge apparently was still at lunch as it was early afternoon. There were approximately twenty people in the court, all African American.

We all sat quietly, Gene holding my hand and Ginger observing everything as she always does. Attorney McDaniel opened his cavernous briefcase and removed papers and a small item. I assumed that was the video. He turned and spoke to some attorneys who were behind him in the room. One was an African American woman dressed in a navy-blue suit. She was petite with black, page style coifed hair. She seemed to be looking for someone, probably her client.

I would later learn that she was for the prosecution and argued that I should be remanded to the grand jury. To think that another African American female would move forward with these ridiculous and obviously malicious charges was beyond me.

With a flash, the atmosphere of the room changed. Doors suddenly opened, a bailiff started moving toward the bench, and a court stenographer breezed in quickly to take their positions.

Knees wobbly at the prospect of facing Detective McHugh again, I thought to myself, please stand. Just looking at him elicited chills. I told God that I knew his power would keep me strong. My attorney and I appeared before Judge Sullivan. I felt more potent knowing the spirit of the Lord was with me. I was not afraid to speak with power and truth.

Judge Sullivan read the arrest warrant that was written by Detective McHugh. McHugh clearly stated that I was 'packing a police semi-automatic weapon and knew that police officers were trying to enter my home, and Gene and I would not let them in.' His warrant was so erroneous even the judge was not trying to believe it. He kept looking up with a curious stare in his eyes.

In all of my seventy-seven years of life, I had never been in such fundamental disbelief. McHugh looked uneasy to me, knowing the lies he wrote to get the arrest warrant. The judge and McDaniel proceeded with the hearing. Attorney McDaniel made his case, requesting that Judge Sullivan review the video. The judge did not wish to review it indicating that it was too grainy, which was delineated in the arrest warrant and that it was too late in the day. Though his requests were polite and respectful, Attorney McDaniel repeatedly insisted that he take the time to look at the video.

Judge Sullivan said, "Rather than the video, a better determination can be made by the claimant appearing in court so a judge can look at her and notice her body language to see if she twists, squirms and turns in her seat."

McHugh testified that I told Simpson I had a gun and waved it. Then I told her that I would give her the barrel of my gun rather than any information concerning myself and insurance. Judge Sullivan ruled the case would be remanded to the Grand Jury, saying there was probable cause. Realizing I would have to wait out this caustic journey to obtain justice, I left the courtroom in tears.

CHAPTER 12

POST-TRAUMATIC STRESS DISORDER

From August 11, 2015, when Judge Sullivan decided to continue my case based on probable cause, sleep was not my friend. Every aspect of my life was suffering and moving slowly towards not having any purpose. I felt like I had a daily nervous breakdown, which was the terminology used by my generation. I did not think my existence could get any worse, but it really did get worse. And it was not the August heat and humidity in DC.

Several days in a row would pass with no sleep, or no more than two to three hours a night filled with worry or bad dreams about being convicted of a crime that I did not commit. All those sleepless nights severely impacted my health.

The nervous feeling in my body, trembling hands, nausea, malaise, anxiety, and depression was overwhelming. Many days, I did not get dressed and sat on the white sofa in our family room. My family would come by to visit me, and I would sit there, not smiling, not eating, not laughing or talking, basically a shell of the woman I once was.

Gene was always by my side. He said, "Vashti, I have observed your actions and you need to go to your medical doctor because you are not doing well."

I countered, "Gene, you need to help yourself."

"Not as bad as you do," he said.

"Are you a doctor, now?" I asked.

"No," he said. "But I know you, and I know how settled and happy you have been in the past."

Needless to say, our marriage took a turn. The joy and happiness in our home disappeared. No matter how hard Gene tried, I could not respond to him the same way as before. There was no hand holding, hugs, gentle kisses, passion—nothing. He was encouraging me that things would get better but was also frustrated that I wouldn't get help. We argued over the smallest things. Before, I had never yelled at Gene, but it seemed like every day I was yelling at him about something.

Looking back, I feel sick thinking about how I must have hurt him. He was hurting too. Those guns were pointed at him on Capitol Hill, too and he had endured being handcuffed in his own home like a common criminal. A proud black man with no criminal record going through this in his golden years. But I could not feel his pain—only my own.

Even Ginger and Danton were suffering. But I was too mired in my own pain to see anyone else's. I was the one who went to jail and might be going back to jail. The thought of it made me want to vomit everything inside of me.

I was so tired of Gene talking about my situation. I finally gave in and said, "Okay, Gene, I'll see our internist."

Gene didn't understand. I knew I needed help. My blood was boiling trying to get out the anger that I felt. I would advise anyone going through what I have experienced to seek advice immediately.

I called and scheduled an appointment with my internist of ten years.

Dr. Kohn took one look at me and said, "Vashti, you don't look well. Before I begin your examination, tell me what is wrong with you."

I said, "Well, Dr. Kohn, I have had a terrible experience that involved false accusations that I assaulted a woman with a gun."

Dr. Kohn said, "This is not believable. I have treated you for a long time and have an airtight opinion of you. This is just plain false."

"Dr. Kohn, my nights are almost sleepless."

She asked how many hours I was sleeping at night, and I guessed and said maybe four. Her medical examination revealed that my blood pressure was way too high, among other things. I wasn't eating well, and when I did eat, it was not homemade food because I was no longer cooking. My internist increased my cholesterol medication and told me to focus on my diet to help control my high blood pressure. She prescribed anxiety medication and sleeping medication.

"Vashti," she said, "we will see if these two medications help ease your anxiety and help you sleep. If not, I will refer you to see a psychiatrist. I need to see you back in a few weeks. However, call me to let me know how you are feeling."

I left her office feeling like I at least had something to help me sleep. In a few weeks, I began to sleep a bit longer, but my anxiety remained the same. I was lethargic and still depressed. Our family tried to keep me occupied by taking me out to dinner, trying to get me to church again, and going to events that we were receiving invitations to in September. Late August and September were filled with essential family, social, and church events for us.

Ginger's birthday is in August, and me and Gene's birthday is in September. Our church takes a summer break, but in September, we celebrate the church's anniversary and other important initiatives such as Feed the 5000, which feeds 5000 families in Northern Virginia. The Congressional Black Caucus Annual Conference is also in September. For many years we have attended meetings, parties, the prayer breakfast, and the gala dinner hosted by Blacks in the US Congress. The President of the United States usually attends the gala dinner as well as many of our friends.

I had no interest in any of this, not even celebrating family birthdays. At Gene's absolute insistence, I did go to our favorite restaurant, The Prime Rib. As October approached, my granddaughter and son's birthday consumed a considerable amount of my family event planning, but frankly, I could not even remember the dates.

I realized that I needed to call Dr. Kohn like she asked me to and let her know that my social life was changing. Gene asked me nearly every day to call her, so I finally picked up the phone and made the call. She called me back, and I filled her in on everything that I was feeling emotionally.

Physically, the medication seemed to be working. I told Dr. Kohn that I was still having problems with my stomach, and she prescribed something to help. She also made a referral to see a psychiatrist named Dr. Richards.

Dr. Richards had two offices, one in Chevy Chase and another in Silver Spring. The first time we met, it was a sunny day in October. Young in appearance, and casual, she had on a beige sweater, jeans, and boots with two-inch heels.

I wore my leather chocolate brown jacket, cashmere beige sweater, and dark brown pants. Because it was getting chilly, I wore my leopard print hat that Ginger gave me for Christmas. I was appropriately dressed, but funky casual for my seventy-seven-year-old self. I was depressed, but not so depressed that I no longer cared about my appearance in public. Somehow, no matter what, I found the energy to pull how I looked together. At home, that was another story.

Dr. Richards's countenance was a tale of two beings, warm but distant, lively yet reserved, focused but detached. I guess that is how psychiatrists are: professional but not personal, with the effort of keeping their distance.

"Mrs. Sherrod, may I call you Vashti, or would you prefer Mrs. Sherrod"? Dr. Richards asked.

I responded, "Please, call me Vashti."

"Your name is very different," she said.

I gave her the background and history of my name and how I got it. We sat together, and she just looked at me for at least five minutes. I thought to myself *this is the creepiest thing I have ever been involved in*. Finally, she said, "I need the family background from you. Tell me briefly what your problem is."

I took a deep breath and shared my ordeal with her—my new identity: Vashti Sherrod, criminal and accused of committing assault with a deadly weapon. I told her that I was feeling alone and no longer had the warm relationship I experienced with my husband, isolation from my friends and church.

After a long period of silence and note-taking, Dr. Richards said, "Vashti, how do you spend your time?"

I thought it an irrelevant question and asked her why. She responded that it was a fundamental question and went to my state of mind. After thoughtfully answering Dr. Richards, she dug into the injury by the claimant and Detective McHugh. I began to cry, it felt like my chest would cave in.

Dr. Richards could see how distraught I'd become, but she did not say anything, so I continued to explain how the pain of what they did hurt me. Sharing with her the traumatic experience of guns being pointed at our heads during the Capitol Hill stop and in our own home unleashed another emotional outburst. The impact of seeing those big weapons that can kill being aimed at me for the first time in my life would never, ever, ever not trigger fear, anxiety, and anger.

For the first time since we met, I saw softness and emotion in Dr. Richards's eyes. She had a look of shock and disbelief.

At the end of our first session, she said she wanted to see me twice a week and then we would go to once a week. "Call me, Vashti, if you need to talk. Let me know if you feel your depression is getting more severe where, for example, you cannot get out of bed or you feel like hurting yourself. We have a lot of work to do to get you feeling better and in control of your life again. We can do that, Vashti, together."

Twice a week for several months, I met with the fortyish year-old white female psychiatrist. I was worried about how she perceived me because of my age, being African American, and the reason I was there. Would she stereotype me? Would she empathize with the claimant?

This is the journey of our people. Never knowing exactly how we are perceived or whether racial stereotypes would rear its ugly head. For seventy-eight years, that has been my journey in life. Carrying the load of racial stigma and assumptions about who I am because of the stealth nature of white supremacy.

This ultimately is how I ended up being accused of such a heinous crime. I learned later that Dr. Richards understood this intuitively. She realized that part of my problem was I had been stripped down to no longer being a person because the claimant's and Detective McHugh's actions stemmed from their racial bias, prejudice, and stereotypes against African Americans.

My realization that nothing like this could have happened to a white person triggered old wounds, fears, and deep anger and resentment hid over my lifetime. These reactions and anxieties were making me sick.

As Dr. Richards and I met each week, I discussed various aspects of my experience with racism. One visit I shared about my ride on the back of the bus from Filbert to York, with my dearly beloved sister. Virginia had returned home on her furlough from the Women's

Army Corp to take my baby brother Ronnie into town for an ice cream cone. We got off the Trailways bus and bought ice cream at the back of the store following the sign for "coloreds only" and looked at the stores on Main Street in York, South Carolina, the county seat. We took in a movie where Blacks followed the signs leading to the balcony. Virginia chuckled and said to her baby sister and baby brother, "Blacks have the best seats."

I told Dr. Richards that Virginia told Daddy that she purposely rode the bus all dressed in her WAC uniform because in her heart, she was serving her country and was in the first group of African American women to serve in the US Army. However, this made no difference to the racism that infected that town. Daddy told us we must fight for change. He said he would continue to fight for justice against racism.

As the visits with Dr. Richards continued, we dug into what was happening to me mentally. We focused on what was causing my depression, anger, and fear that Detective

McHugh would kill us for no reason other than we were middle-class African Americans who lived in Mitchellville. Dr. Richards diagnosed my condition as Post Traumatic Stress Disorder, which is a disorder that prevents sufferers from recovering after experiencing a traumatic event. Triggers bring back memories of the trauma, along with severe emotional and physical reactions. All my symptoms fit within those of PTSD sufferers, according to Dr. Richards.

Treatment with her was exactly how to get the PTSD under control, and the outcome of our sessions was to apply her techniques to gain control when events triggered a relapse. I kept a list of techniques with me everywhere I went, and I tried to read the list every day. I would take deep breaths and go over the most useful actions I could take. The most beneficial technique to prevent triggers was to avoid television news and negative conversations. I also employed mental imagery techniques to view the situation in a new way so that I could gain control of my life. Stressful memories trigger the symptoms of PTSD, so it was vital to avoid places and situations that brought back painful memories. To that end, I also made a list of stressful memories from my life, particularly discrimination experienced in my life.

I have always been afraid of guns. Avoiding movies, news, or anything about guns would reduce triggers and fears that resurrected the horror of unscrupulous police officers or individuals. Even seeing police officers in cars, or walking close to them, triggers my PTSD. So, I had to create new imagery in my mind when I see police officers. Instead of thinking about Detective McHugh and what happened to me, I needed to consciously think about police officers who help seniors, protect children on the way to school, or participate positively in community events.

After several weeks of working with Dr. Richards, I was retraining how I think about police officers, guns, and white women. It did not always work, but I tried. As I evolved in my therapy, I shared her advice with Gene,

Ginger, and Danton. Often it was hard to find someone to confide in, but we had each other. And spending time with those who knew what happened helped.

We released the stress of trying to keep our lives in order by getting household help, eating out more, and lightening our load. We also took short walks in our neighborhood and tried some breathing and relaxation techniques I learned. We did not return to church, concerts, or events with crowds because of the triggers that might occur.

I was trying to reclaim my strength so that I could return to the wife that I once was and restore my marriage to how we lived before May 15, 2015. That date would forever be branded in my memory, the day that started this journey. A journey that I never thought would ever be mine. Now a second date, August 11, 2015, was embellished on my heart. The day probable cause came knocking on my door. And every year, these dates trigger depression and sadness in my spirit. I will never, ever forget.

CHAPTER 13

The Call

I existed day-to-day, sitting in my family room looking out the window while trying to avoid TV news. The phone rang, and it was Attorney McDaniel.

"Hi, Mrs. Sherrod, how are you doing?" he asked.

I responded, "I am not well but trying to keep myself together."

"I am sorry to hear that, but I just wanted to call and check on you and Mr. Sherrod."

"Thank you, we appreciate that. I will let him know. Do you have any news?"

"No, none yet. When the grand jury meets, we will not know. Everything is done in secret. The court will issue the decision, and then we will learn what we need to do. I need to let you know, Mrs. Sherrod, that sometimes it takes many months before we hear anything from them."

My heart sank. "How long do you think it will take, Attorney McDaniel?"

"It could take anywhere from three to six months. Usually, not longer than that."

"I do not think I can make it that long. That means at a minimum, I will have to go through October, November, and December?"

"Yes," he said. "Just try to be patient and take care of yourself and Mr. Sherrod."

"Thank you for the call."

"Bye, Mrs. Sherrod, take care."

I hung up the phone and called out to Gene.

"Vash, what is wrong?" he asked.

I could not stop crying. He held me in his arms, and I told him that Attorney McDaniel said it might take three to six months before we heard anything from the court. I would live with this weight on my heart every day.

Late autumn was usually one of the happiest times of the year for me. But that no longer held true. I was relieved daylight savings time had ended. The fact that mother nature darkened earlier than summer, forced by a move of turning the clock back an hour, meant I didn't have to stare out the window wondering whether I was going to jail or not. With the weather rainy and cold and the leaves changing colors, I went to bed around 5 p.m. when it turned dark. But lying in bed gave me more time to worry and think about what could be coming to me.

Memories of celebrating Thanksgiving and Christmas holidays, which are longstanding family traditions, flooded my mind. With joy, my hands worked hard to fill our home with all the finery and beauty possible. I often decorated with two Christmas trees. My eight-to-ten-foot trees had a collection of ornaments obtained over many years. We hosted both Thanksgiving and Christmas dinner in our home, and I prided myself on putting my heart into each dish and cooking the best meal. I would spend hours planning the meal, and of course, if we had a Christmas party, that too.

When my sister Virginia lived in Washington, she often hosted the holiday dinner. As it should be, since I was the remaining female on the Sanders side in the area, I joyfully held the rights to host family holiday events.

With no energy to focus on the holidays, my depression worsened. Knowing the grand jury would be coming together at any time to decide my fate, my nerves knotted in a ball. Imagine living in such torment, daily wondering if the grand jury would decide to move forward with prosecuting a senior citizen on an assault with deadly weapon charge.

The day I spent in jail still haunted me. And the thought of going for years numbed my body and my mind to where I could not think. With each passing day, as we waited to hear the outcome of the grand jury, I worried and worried more. Even looking at my list from Dr. Richards didn't really help me.

Every day I walked to the mailbox hoping the court had sent a letter exonerating me of this horrible accusation, freeing me from my nightmare. That daily activity was the only time I left the house other than to see Dr. Richards, my internist, or going out with our family to dinner, a movie, or the salon. My family was determined to get me out of the house and help me stay as active as possible. They didn't give me a choice about dinner or a movie; they would not take no for an answer. But every day, my trek to the mailbox was like a spiritual journey.

I likened the trek to being on the underground railroad. Each step was a step towards freedom. I was imprisoned in my own home until the decision was rendered, and each day my red mailbox was my hope to freedom. I would open the lid to the box, and my heart would race as I sorted through the mail. Sometimes, when no letter appeared in the box, tears would stream down my face.

Under Ginger's wise counsel to be cautious, I would stand to the side of the mailbox in case something was in it that would injure me. I wasn't sure who my enemies were or who in my life might want to hurt me.

Almost a week before Thanksgiving, I knew I could not host dinner. Thankfully, Ginger and Danton agreed to do it. Ginger is such a dutiful daughter and did her best to keep me sane. She really wanted to stay with the plan and not deviate from our family's tradition, but she decided because of my emotional state to have us over for the long weekend without any other family. She was doing everything she could to keep me from falling into the abyss. We enjoy Thanksgiving so much that we often do a contest on a favorite recipe to see who does a better job preparing the dish. But I was in no shape to do that. I was lucky to make it to their home.

Driving to Mount Vernon is always lovely, particularly in the fall. The parkway, with its view of the Potomac River, is lined with beautiful old trees. We enjoyed a quiet drive taking in the calming scenery. Eagles' nests could be seen in the trees as Canadian geese and a blue heron nestled in the woods. The fall foliage was gorgeous with reds, yellows, oranges, and mixed hues on a wide variety of trees from oak to red maple to dogwoods. Lost in the picturesque beauty of nature, I briefly forgot about our ordeal, about the grand jury, or what might happen to me.

As we turned down Ginger's street, I felt sad but happy. Sad because so much time had passed since we last visited, and happy because yellow mums adorned her manicured yard which accented the colorful trees and a beautiful wreath with fall foliage hung on her front door. I was proud of my daughter. Her home was beautiful, and this brought a smile to my face.

Pulling into the driveway, I could see both she and Danton in the doorway, smiling. They came out to greet us on the sidewalk and helped us into the house with all our luggage.

"Happy Thanksgiving, Mommy!" Ginger said.

As we entered the house, I could smell freshly baked pies, sweet potato, I hoped, and other foods. Gene and Danton did their usual handshaking and back slaps as we all headed into the family room. We began to talk, and I walked to the window to look at their enormous backyard. "Your yard is beautiful," I said. Then I broke out into tears.

"What's wrong, Mommy?"

I could not speak. The yard triggered thoughts of how much I had missed and that I might be imprisoned.

What would we do?

Thanksgiving dinner was excellent. Gene and I needed those four days from home. It was the first time we'd left our home for an extended overnight except to go down into the basement to sleep when we feared Detective McHugh or to stay at the Hyatt Regency for a court appearance.

When we returned home, I parked the car in the garage and headed to the mailbox. Holding my breath, I began to sweat even though it was cold. I opened the mailbox. There was mail, but nothing from the court. As soon as we entered the house, I rushed to check the voicemail to see if I had missed a call from Attorney McDaniel. Nothing.

No messages. It was December and still no call from the court. Per our family tradition, we begin planning for the Christmas holiday at Thanksgiving. We decide who is hosting all the events around Christmas, and we randomly draw names from a basket for our Christmas gift exchange. We started this years ago as the family grew and buying everyone a gift became impractical. Laughter and giggles accompany this family event while we eat sweet potato pie and ice cream. This year was different. I told everyone that I did not have the energy or desire to celebrate Christmas.

Gene, Ginger, and Danton met my eyes with silence and stares. I knew they were all shocked, this was not me. Not celebrate Christmas. This was not in my DNA. This was an imposter. Not Vashti, believer in Christ Jesus. The happiest time of year for me was to celebrate his birth. Not put up a Christmas tree or decorate the house. Not Vashti. They all weighed in, encouraging me to not let the claimant and Detective McHugh stop me from celebrating Christmas. It was my turn this year, but I could not do it. Not like this.

Mid December arrived, but no news. I continued to check the mail every day. Sometimes even twice a day. Even the cold temperatures did not stop me from going to that mailbox. My anxiety ramped up so much, I thought maybe I should start calling the court. I initiated a query to determine the telephone number of the department that would send the letter out to notify the accused of the grand jury's decision and found a direct contact into that department.

He was a supervisor, professional and a very kind individual.

"Hello," I said. "My name is Vashti Sherrod, and I have been waiting for the decision from the grand jury regarding my case."

He asked for the case number.

"It is 623-242893."

"Thank you, hold for a minute, please."

I called again.

"This is Mr. Hamilton."

"Oh hello, Mr. Hamilton. This is Vashti Sherrod, we spoke a few days ago about my case."

"Yes, I recall. I haven't received any new information about your case, Mrs. Sherrod."

"Would it be okay if I call you directly rather than going through the switchboard?"

"Yes, certainly. My number is 202-xxx-xxxx. You may call me anytime. I understand that you are anxious to get information. We do send a letter, as you know."

"Yes, I check the mailbox every day. I appreciate that you have no problem with me calling you directly."

"These things do take time, Mrs. Sherrod. We do not know where the grand jury is until we receive the decision in our office. But do continue to call and check your mail for communication from us."

And I did just that. I kept checking my mail daily and calling him two to three times each week. Mr. Hamilton was always patient and always kind. Eventually, I told him what happened to me. As much as he could show it, he was empathetic and sympathetic. I will never forget his kindness.

Dr. Richards tried to get me to reconsider

my decision to not celebrate Christmas. "Vashti, this holiday is significant to you, spiritually and socially. If you do not celebrate it, the impact on your depression may be significant."

I asked her why she believed that.

She said, "Well, it is part of your history, your family life, and your good memories. You may grow to associate this decision with the negative events of the past and may forever have triggers related to the Christmas you didn't celebrate."

She'd offered me some things to pray about and discuss with Gene that I hadn't before considered. I told her I would think about what she said.

"Good, Vashti, I think that is a great decision, and whatever you decide, it will empower you either way because you will have thought through the positive and negative impacts carefully."

I really enjoyed talking to Dr. Richards. She was a blessing. I did not carefully think about

Christmas for several days. If I was going to do anything, I needed to get busy.

"I had a dream last night." We were lying in bed and I looked over at Gene.

"What was it?" he asked.

"Well, I had a dream about Christmas, and we were so happy. I could see the tree and gifts and the kids and their faces. Dr. Richards was right. Christmas memories are to be cherished and not tainted or infected by this nightmare. We should always look back on them as special because we are celebrating the birth of our Lord and Savior, Jesus Christ. You know what, Gene? We are going to host Christmas for the family. It won't be like in the past, but we are going to do it."

"Okay, darling."

"Wow, you haven't called me that in a long time." My heart smiled, and for the first time in a long while, I felt in control. I created a checklist in my mind of all that needed to be done. I needed to get out the Christmas decorations and make a shopping list. I could order gifts online, but I needed to go to the market on Capitol Hill. I could not wait to call Ginger.

"Hello, Ginger."

"Hi, Mommy, how are you today?"

"I am simply fine."

"Really? Awesome!"

"Well, Ginger, I have decided that I am going to host Christmas!"

"That is fantastic news!" Ginger responded. "I cannot believe it. I am so happy."

"Well, we only have two weeks before Christmas, so I better get going."

"Is there anything I can do, Mommy?"

"Yes, let's cook Christmas Eve and Christmas Day dinner together. I cannot do all of that."

"Of course, I can do that. Let's make a list of what we are going to cook. I can also help decorate the house. Let's go this weekend to get the Christmas tree!"

And that is what we did. We all got together and went to Homestead Gardens in Annapolis, Maryland, to buy a Christmas tree, poinsettias, garlands, wreaths, and all the traditional items we purchase.

It had been quite a while since we all felt this happy, but the cloud was not far away. I pushed it away anytime it came near me and devoted my energy to Christmas. My therapy and prayer helped me deal with whatever I had to face.

By the time we arrived home from our outing, I was exhausted. The kids placed everything in the house and started on the decorations and tree. We decided to make a weekend of it because I was so behind. I made my daily trek to the mailbox and there was nothing. But this time, I was not going to get depressed. The aroma of Christmas permeated the house bringing back so many happy and beautiful memories. By the end of the weekend, everything was up and gorgeous.

Danton put Christmas lights on the trees and shrubbery. Neighbors who passed by would take pictures and let their kids sit under our sparkling evergreens at night. This gave me joy for a time. After Christmas and New

Year's Eve, I settled back into the reality that 2016, would start with a cloud over my head.

I still had not received a decision from the court, and my sojourn to the mailbox and calls to the court continued. One day, I called the court.

"Hello, may I speak to Mr. Hamilton," I said.

"Yes, this is he."

"Oh. Hi, Mr. Hamilton, this is Vashti Sherrod calling to see if there is any news about my case."

"I will check, Mrs. Sherrod, hold on a minute, please."

I waited about two minutes before he returned to the phone.

"Mrs. Sherrod, I do have news. We have the decision about your case."

I held my breath and began to shake.

"The grand jury did not bring charges against you. I repeat, the grand jury did not bring any charges against you. The case has been dismissed."

I could not believe my ears.

"Gene! Gene!" I called out. "Thank you so

much, Mr. Hamilton. Oh my God, Praise the Lord. Thank you, Jesus!"

"I know you are thrilled, and I am happy for you," Mr. Hamilton said. "You will receive a letter in a few days, and when you receive that letter, you need to come to our office so we can close out the file."

"Oh, yes, I will be there as soon as I receive the letter. Thank you so much for your support."

"You are welcome, Mrs. Sherrod. I can feel your smile through the phone."

Gene came into the family room, and we embraced. Tears streamed down our faces. Joyful tears. January 6, 2016, would be another day to add to this horrible journey, but it was the best day of my life since May 15, 2015. The day I learned of my total vindication. The phone rang, and I looked at the caller ID. It was Attorney McDaniel calling to share what I already knew.

Bless him.

THE McDANIEL LAW GROUP, P.L.L.C.
ATTORNEYS AT LAW
1920 L Street NW, Suite #303, Washington, DC 20036
Telephone (202)331-0793 • Facsimile (202)331-7004 (202) 765-2250

Brian K. McDaniel, Esq.
brianmac1911@aol.com
Admitted in DC, MD & WA

Nesiboch A. St. Hill, Esq.
nesiboch@gmail.com
Admitted in MD & DC

January 15, 2016

VIA HAND-DELIVERY
D.C. Office of Risk Management
Attn: Claims Bureau
441 4th Street, N.W., Suite 800 South
Washington D.C. 20001

Mayor Muriel Bowser
1350 Pennsylvania Avenue, N.W.,
Washington D.C. 20004

Re: Modified Notice of Claim: False Report, Malicious Prosecution, False Arrest, Harassment and Intentional Infliction of Emotional Distress

Claimant: *Vashti ▬▬ Sherrod*
▬ Lake Front Drive
Mitchellville, Maryland 20721

Date of Incident: *July 20, 2015*

Time of Incident: *Began in and around the early morning hours of July 20, 2015*

Location of Incident: *▬ Lake Front Drive, Mitchellville, Maryland 20721and the First District Police precinct 500 E. Street, S.E. Washington D.C.*

To Whom It May Concern:

Pursuant to D.C. Code § 12-309, this letter is to provide notice of claim and to advise you that The McDaniel Law Group, P.L.L.C. will represent the claimant, Vashti ▬▬ Sherrod, in connection with a false report that was filed against her by Detective Phillip J. McHugh and the ensuing harassment which led to her false arrest and the malicious prosecution.

On or before June 29, 2015 Detective Phillip McHugh falsely reported that the vehicle belonging to Mrs. Sherrod was stolen so that local law enforcement would stop the vehicle on sight. On June 29, 2015, after the vehicle was stopped based upon Detective McHugh's false report, Detective McHugh executed a search of Mrs. Sherrod's

1

vehicle and did not find a firearm. On July 7, 2015, officers of the Metropolitan Police Department, including Detective Phillip J. McHugh, executed a search warrant at the home of Mrs. Sherrod located at 920 Lake Front Drive, Mitchellville, Maryland 20721 in the early hours of the morning. As a result of the search no firearm was recovered. Based on Detective McHugh's affidavit in support of an arrest warrant for Mrs. Sherrod which was filled with information that Detective McHugh knew to be untrue and/or inaccurate or at least should have known that the information was untrue and/or inaccurate, Mrs. Sherrod was arrested at the First District Station and transported to Central Cell Block in the District of Columbia. Mrs. Sherrod was held for several hours before she was finally taken before Judge Renee Raymond. At this hearing, Mrs. Sherrod was informed that she was being charged with Assault With A Dangerous Weapon and was released. The case was captioned as United States of America v. Vashti Sherrod with case number 2015 CF2 009738.

Subsequent to her release, Mrs. Sherrod was forced to secure counsel at her expense to defend against the false claims. On January 6, 2016, after having the aforementioned case hanging over her head almost six (6) months, the case was dismissed at the behest of the government.

Additionally, Detective McHugh sponsored an arrest warrant which contained claims made by a civilian witness that he knew not to be true. Specifically, the civilian witness alleged that Mrs. Sherrod pointed a firearm at it on or about May 14, 2015. Detective McHugh was in possession of a surveillance videotape, prior to the request for the arrest warrant, that evidenced that the claims of the civilian witness were not true. Detective McHugh pursued the arrest of Mrs. Sherrod irrespective of the contrary evidence which was in his possession.

Mrs. Sherrod endured financial expenses by having to hire counsel to defend against these false allegations which could have been avoided if not for the false affidavit submitted by Detective Phillip J. McHugh. Moreover, Mrs. Sherrod experienced emotional distress, embarrassment and disparagement by having officers come to her home and ransack the same for all her neighbors to see. Mrs. Sherrod believes that the District of Columbia is responsible for the injuries she sustained as a result of Detective McHugh's actions and that she should be compensated for those injuries.

As stated earlier, this correspondence serves as the Mrs. Sherrod's notice in compliance with the D.C. Code § 12-309 and is also being filed within the six month time period.

Should you have any questions or concerns or wish to discuss this matter further, please feel free to contact us at your convenience.

Very truly yours,

Brian K. McDaniel, Esq.
Counsel for Mrs. Sherrod

2

CHAPTER 14

RECLAMATION

My days became more peaceful. I felt like I was getting my power back. The day after finding out the grand jury had dropped all charges and exonerated me, my breathing felt somewhat normal. I could not discern any butterflies in my stomach.

My entire focus was on getting that letter from the deputy clerk's office in black and white. Gene and I arrived to wall-to-wall people standing, sitting, and coming in and out of various doors. We took our place in line, which seemed to wrap around for a mile. I could see behind what appeared to be bulletproof glass with a small hole and a silver speaker mounted at eye-level. Most of the people in line were much younger than I.

"Vash, is there another line?" Gene asked. "This one sure is long."

"Gene, this is the right place. Be patient."

Finally, we got to the front of the line, and I flashed my smile at the gentleman behind the glass wall. "Hi, I am Vashti Sherrod, and I am here to see Mr. Hamilton."

"Just a minute," he responded. "Please have a seat, Mrs. Sherrod, and I will get him."

Gene and I sat down, then I became anxious. What if something goes wrong? What if Mr. Hamilton is not here today? My mind started getting a bit paranoid. Just sitting there gave me flashbacks of court. I no longer had a good feeling. I could not come back here again. Triggers. Triggers.

"Mrs. Sherrod, we are ready for you," a gentleman said.

I jumped up quickly and got back in line. He waved me to the front of the line.

"Hi, my name is Mr. Myers, Mrs. Sherrod."

"Where is Mr. Hamilton," I asked.

"Oh, Mr. Hamilton is not here right now."

I was disappointed, I had spoken to him often regarding my case. "Mr. Myers, can you please tell him 'thank you' from me for all his support?"

A door opened behind Mr. Myers, and he turned around to see who was behind him. "Hey, Hamilton! I thought you were off this afternoon," said Mr. Myers.

"No, man," Mr. Hamilton responded. "I was in a meeting that went long."

Mr. Myers gave him an update about why I was there.

"Well, hello, Mrs. Sherrod," Mr. Hamilton said. "We have talked off and on the past few months. I am glad you were able to make it down here to pick up your exoneration paperwork. This is a great day for you, and me too, actually. I am happy for you."

I gave him a big smile. I think every tooth in my head was showing.

"Wow, what a beautiful smile you have," he said. "I had a particularly good feeling about you. Let me go to my office to retrieve your paperwork."

I was still smiling as he walked away. My heart smiled. My face smiled. My soul smiled.

Mr. Hamilton was warm each time I spoke to him. I think he knew in his heart that I was innocent. I must have called him twenty times between August and yesterday. He was always patient, kind, and professional. Just what I, and the world, needed.

"Mrs. Sherrod, here is the paperwork, and most importantly the letter exonerating you from these charges and getting your record expunged. The attached form, along with your signature, is simply something we need for our records to indicate you received the letter. Just fill out the top portion, and sign and date it."

As I reviewed the document, tears started streaming down my face. There was no, "I'm sorry," or "terrible inconvenience, here's your $15,000 for legal fees back." Absolutely nothing like that. Just a form stating that the case was dismissed 'with prejudice,' whatever that meant.

Still, I was happy. I took my pen and executed the document. As I handed the form back, my eyes met Mr. Hamilton's. I wiped away my tears thinking about how much it took to get to this point. An entire year of my life lost because I wanted to go buy flowers for our yard.

"Mrs. Sherrod, I wish you the best. Do you have any questions?"

"Well, yes, Mr. Hamilton. We spent a lot of money in legal fees. How do I get a refund on those costs?"

"Mrs. Sherrod, you will need to fill out this claim form. But I think there is a limit," Mr. Hamilton said.

"A limit? Thank you for the form." I took one look at the form and decided it would not be something I would fill out without speaking to Attorney McDaniel. I thanked him again and left.

I was angry that after all we had been through, we needed to initiate the process of getting our money back. I thought the District would automatically reach out and render their apologies and offer to refund our costs in this matter.

"Gene, let's go!"

"Vash, you sound frustrated," he said.

"I am. We must fill out a form to request a refund for all we spent in legal fees. It just doesn't seem fair."

Gene responded, "You need to call Attorney McDaniel when we get home."

"Okay, I will, as soon as we get home."

When we arrived home, I picked up the phone to call Attorney McDaniel on his cell phone.

He answered on the first ring. "Attorney McDaniel."

"Good afternoon, Attorney McDaniel. This is Mrs. Sherrod. I am calling to let you know that I have the release papers from the court. We just got back a few minutes ago."

"Well, congratulations, Mrs. Sherrod. I am happy to hear that you and Mr. Sherrod were able to get downtown to get your release paperwork," Attorney McDaniel responded.

"Thank you, we need to drop them off to you and discuss how we are going to get a refund for our legal fees."

"Yes, why don't we meet in my office at a

time convenient for you. Just call my secretary to schedule an appointment."

"I will call her now, Attorney McDaniel."

"Great. Have a good evening."

I made an appointment to meet with Attorney McDaniel the following day.

Gene suggested we get the family together and go to the Prime Rib, our usual restaurant for celebrating special events. I called Ginger to see if she and Danton would be available for dinner at 7 p.m. If so, they could meet us after our late afternoon meeting with Attorney McDaniel. Ginger texted back: Yes, we are available.

I felt a sense of relief. Perhaps tomorrow we would be able to get the ball rolling to get our legal fees refunded and we would celebrate my release from the most horrific experience of my life. The refund wouldn't give me back my mental health status, or my feeling that justice had been served, but at least I'd feel like we didn't give the District government our hard-earned money to assault our constitutional rights and liberties.

"Good evening, Mr. and Mrs. Sherrod. It is good to see you. Right this way."

"It is good to see you too, James" I responded.

The Prime Rib was our favorite place to eat, and the maître d', Larry, had been like family. But he had no idea what I had been through. All our ups and downs, highs and lows. We had not shared this experience with anyone outside of our family. Jail? Arrested? Never. Even though I was totally innocent, to be tarnished like that filled me with deep shame. People would never believe it.

Larry led us to our favorite table where Ginger and Danton waited.

The restaurant was gorgeous. Painted black walls trimmed in gold with leopard-print carpet. Huge flower arrangements surrounded the room, along with lithographs and paintings hand-stenciled with various poses of nude women. Our favorite table had two high-back tufted leather chairs and two short chairs directly across. Gene and I always sat across from each other as did Ginger and Danton. Ginger and I sat side by side.

Ginger jumped up when she saw us. "Hi, Mommy and Dada! I am so glad to see you." Hugs and kisses ensued.

Danton rose to greet us. "Hey, Gene, today is a day to celebrate. Dinner is on me!"

They both chuckled. As a family, we knew when Danton volunteered to pay it was a special occasion. My son-in-law worked as a patent attorney at the US Patent and Trademark Office. He and Ginger met there in the late '90s. I felt so bad that he'd had to endure this ridiculous situation.

Sadly, white Americans do not really know the struggle of African Americans until it is right in their face, and the acknowledgment of the struggle moves beyond stories from history or from local news in a very real and personal way.

We all took a seat and began to banter and have fun. I felt much better now that the nightmare was behind me.

"So, Mommy, how was the meeting with Attorney McDaniel?" Ginger asked.

A smile curled onto my lips. "Attorney McDaniel is going to send a letter to the mayor of DC to request directly that all legal fees be refunded by the city. He also filed a formal request through the district court, as well as a request to expunge all records related to the criminal case. "Hopefully, we will win!"

We studied the familiar menu while waiting for our waiter to take our order. I decided to have lobster, as did Ginger. Gene ordered his usual full-cut prime rib, medium-well; and Danton ordered the crab cakes. Generally, we were not a family that drinks, but everyone decided to imbibe. A toast to celebrate the occasion was in order! As the drinks arrived, we all lifted glasses of gin and tonic, margaritas, and olive martinis as high as our arms could reach.

"A toast," Gene announced. "To my beautiful, strong, incredible wife who has survived this struggle with God at her side. Where would we be without the Lord to sustain her?"

"Here, here," Danton seconded.

"Yes," Ginger added, "to my Warrior Mother whose veins are filled with steel!"

Tears flowed from my eyes. I was blessed with a beautiful, supportive, loving family.

Hors d' oeuvres arrived as the jazz ensemble played all the favorite standards from our time. Gene ordered a red wine and held it as elegantly as he always does. "Let's get down to business."

"Gene, I thought we were celebrating tonight. Business is over." Always the businessman, I thought.

"No, Vash," Gene said, "it's time to seek legal assistance to get justice for you so that you will be whole again."

"Gene, this is the first night in a long time that I haven't felt anxious or depressed. I just want to relax tonight. Ginger, Danton, all of us need to relax for once."

"Well, I tell you what," Ginger said, "I am going to do some research and talk to my friends about getting a lawyer to file a suit for their unscrupulous use of power to take a white woman's word against two senior citizens. Clearly, this was a racially based practice of discrimination and just pure racism."

Danton nodded his head in agreement.

"Okay," I said, "let's start in the morning."

Gene's convincing words and Ginger's desire to engage friends and research the internet to find the right attorney to represent us felt like the right way to go. But that evening, I didn't want to think too much about it. I wanted to sleep.

CHAPTER 15

CIVIL WAR

When I sat up in bed the next morning, I looked around my bedroom and had an epiphany. My skin crawled at the thought of Detective McHugh in my bedroom, in my private space, going through my dresser drawers, clothes, jewelry box, and other personal items. My makeup table with my medications, trinkets, box of favorite nail polish were all so personal. I could feel his spirit in the bedroom. A tear dropped down my cheek and I shivered thinking that he touched the bed I slept in. The night after the raid, I could not feel my body when I entered my bedroom. That same anxiety was overtaking me. I did not think I would ever get over what happened to me.

Gene was right. We needed to fight for our civil rights. The fight for social justice continued to be part of living as an African American in this country. If I let this moment go, I would be complicit in the status quo, allowing racism to permeate our souls and the unscrupulous police to continue injuring African Americans. Just when I thought it would not happen to me, here I was in my own bedroom almost one year after a white woman accused me of brandishing a semi-automatic weapon at her while buying flowers. Flowers!

I laid back down in my bed to pray. Lord, what should I do? Where should I go? Should I continue seeking justice, not just for myself, but for everyone? Should I, Lord, seek to bring light to what happened to us so that others wouldn't have to go through a similar experience? I am waiting on you, Lord, to give me the answer. What is the answer, Lord?

And like a mighty wind, he answered my prayer just that quickly. I felt it in my spirit! He spoke straight to my soul and directed me to move forward. To join the moral universe, which is long and bends that arc towards justice as Dr. Martin Luther King said. "Get up my daughter," he said, "and get on that path of righteousness to help the meek, the poor, those who find themselves wrapped up in this justice system without resources, or family, or friends, to get them through. Those who end up losing their kids, and apartments, and jobs because of the overzealous, mean spirited evil that resides in the hearts of police officers and judges, and lawyers. Humanity needs to stand up to protect those who cannot protect themselves. This country's civil rights laws were founded on the principle that a person is innocent until proven guilty, not the other way around.

As I laid on my pillow in a pool of tears, I also thought about my husband Gene. The tears he poured out, and how he suffered through this not even being able to fully see. The humility and shame of having his home broken into by police offers and being stopped on Capitol Hill. A place of pride for us having been business owners and lifelong residents of the District of Columbia, where many of our clients lived. Some just a few blocks from where we were stopped with shotguns pointed at our heads.

I began to think about how it impacted Ginger also. She stepped in and cooked, cleaned, shopped, took us out to dinner, me to the spa, anything she could do to lift our spirits. My depression restricted my ability to drive, especially in the District of Columbia because I was banned from going into the city. My record might come up from the observation cameras all around the city, and the police might come. If that were to happen, I would never have recovered. So, she drove us to our doctor's appointments at Georgetown and George Washington Universities, to my gynecologist in Bethesda, and to my psychiatrist appointment in upper Northwest Washington, near the National Institute of Health.

Thinking about it made me mad. Our family had been attacked because of the actions of a white woman on Capitol Hill and her unscrupulous police officer. Sometimes I wonder if she and McHugh were friends or dating. I do know that her husband was a high-level individual at the Heritage Foundation in DC. I am sure they had connections at many levels.

A lawsuit would be filed against the claimant and a Metropolitan police officer, and the District of Columbia. Yes, Lord! Give me the strength. I wiped away my tears and jumped out of bed. Thank you, Lord!

As soon as I showered and dressed, I went downstairs to eat breakfast then contacted Attorney McDaniel about the status of our request to get a refund from the District. After speaking to him, I learned that he had written a letter to the mayor of the District of Columbia, Muriel Bowser and planned to hand deliver it to her today. The purpose of the letter was to notify the mayor about the case, and that I had been exonerated. Moreover, Attorney McDaniel requested that all monies paid for legal fees be returned to us.

I cried when I read his letter. Surely, the mayor would respond favorably, especially as a Black woman to another Black woman. Surely, it would prick her heart that senior citizens with a record of community service, professional standing in the District, lifelong adherence to the laws of the United States, and a wife, mother, grandmother, sister, friend to many, and most importantly, a church-going sanctified Baptist believer and worker in my church could be targeted for such grave injustice. I knew when Attorney McDaniel sat down with her and presented the criminal charges and the police misconduct, she would be appalled. Ginger thought she would write a letter of apology and work to refund our legal fees.

We waited for several weeks, and then months, and never received a response from her office. To this day, I remain in disbelief at the coldness and lack of compassion from her and the Office of the Attorney General, Karl Racine.

We started the arduous process of looking for a lawyer to represent us in our civil case. Attorney McDaniel made it clear that he could not represent us in that regard. He never said why, but later, I realized the case would be extraordinarily complex and require a substantial financial investment to work until the case was settled or went to trial. Gene and I called our friends for recommendations and it was a dead end. Ginger loved to conduct research using all types of information systems including the Internet, LexisNexis, Westlaw, and other resources she told me about. Skills she'd learned working in the Patent Office for many years. I was anxious about her findings and looked forward to her call.

"Hello."

"Hi, Mommy how are you doing?"

"I am fine, Ginny (sometimes I called Ginger Ginny). How is the research progressing?"

"Well, I'm making good progress. I have about thirty-five pages of firms specializing in police civil cases. Some I've heard of and some, I have not."

"Okay, that sounds good. I think we should split the list in half. You make some calls, and I will make some."

"Great, Mommy. I will send you your portion by fax, so you can get started quickly."

I received the fax in about ten minutes and looked it over. Many of the firms were in DC and a few in Maryland. I began to call them one-by-one. I was able to get in touch directly with an intake attorney for about eight of the firms in one day. Each intake attorney asked a series of questions, and after I explained the charges and that the grand jury had dropped them, I got dead silence. The violation of my civil rights and liberties was clear, but the issue each had was that police officers have immunity, and the case would require an inordinate amount of legal research, production of discovery including depositions, and could potentially go to trial. I learned quickly that police cases are viewed as time intensive and require a significant investment of resources. I grew increasingly frustrated and stressed hearing that my case was a remarkably interesting civil rights case, but "sorry, we are unable to invest in a police case at this time." My anxiety level was rising, so I decided to stop and focus on another task.

A few days passed, and Ginger called. "Hi,

Mommy, good news. I think I found a law firm!"

"Really? Good!"

"I called about twenty firms, and this one was the last firm. I am looking at their website right now. The firm is Bynum and Jenkins. They are in Alexandria, Virginia. Actually, they are not too far from me and Danton."

"Great, Ginger! Great! I will call them right away."

We needed to file a claim as soon as possible so as to not miss the statute of limitations in the District. I believe the mayor's office was aware that we would be unable to file a claim if we passed that deadline. It was a dirty trick.

I called out to Gene who came downstairs quickly so that we could make the phone call together. I gave him an update, briefing about the firm, so we were on the same page. Unfortunately, we got the firm's voicemail and had to leave a message to return our call.

"Vash, they don't have a receptionist, it must be a small law firm. I am not sure we should go small."

"Gene, the large firms have billable hours at $600 for a partner and $400 for a junior. Do we want to spend that much money on this?"

"Yes," Gene said. "It will be worth it to get justice for you."

We decided to have lunch and hoped that Attorney Bynum would call before we left the house. The phone rang as I was about to take the first bite of my tuna fish sandwich. I ran to grab it before it went to voicemail. "Hello."

"Yes, hello. Is this Mrs. Sherrod? This is Attorney Bynum from Bynum and Jenkins returning your call."

I exhaled a sigh of relief. Hopefully, he did not hear it. "Yes, thank you for returning our call. My husband and I are looking for a law firm to take a civil rights case involving the District and the Metropolitan Police Department." I sounded smart to me. I had spoken to ten intake attorneys, so I had the vernacular down.

"Mrs. Sherrod, it sounds like you and your husband have had an exceedingly difficult experience with MPD. I am sorry to hear this has happened to you both. Please tell me all about it."

I took a deep breath to control my emotions and laid out the case from the beginning to end. He listened carefully and did not interrupt. I really appreciated that. He was also the first attorney who used the word 'sorry.' In my spirit, I hoped he would take our case. After I explained everything that had happened, he asked a few questions about Gene and me, then we scheduled an appointment to meet with him in person at his office in Alexandria.

While we had not resumed our usual activities, from January 6th until the time we met with our new attorney, our lives went on in a new normal. Gene was basically returning to himself, but he would cry if we discussed any aspect of what happened from May 15, 2015 to January 6, 2016. I was still nowhere near myself, with ups and downs that I could not predict. I was still having trouble sleeping and returning to my normal life. I did not think that I ever would. My therapist, Dr. Richards, remained helpful as I tried to restore my confidence, reduce anxiety, and establish trust again.

CHAPTER 16

THE LAWSUIT

We met Attorney Bynum almost one month later, February 2016. I dressed in a black St. John pantsuit with a bright mustard-yellow ruffled blouse. Gene matched the color of his tie and handkerchief to pick up my accent colors. We always dressed to complement each other. It was freezing as we prepared to leave the house, so I grabbed my full-length Black-Gama mink coat and matching hat. The wind was about thirty miles an hour with snow drifts rising from the six inches of snow on the ground. Thankfully, the streets were clear as we headed from Bowie to Alexandria.

I rehearsed in my head the questions Attorney Bynum might ask. I started getting nervous because I did not have much knowledge about him or his firm other than what we could glean from our one phone call. However, my investigator daughter had done some digging and shared that he had worked as a prosecutor for the District of Columbia, graduated from Howard Law School, and did a lot of community work pro bono. Apparently, he also worked as an attorney for a Baptist church in the area. This criterion boosted Ginger's confidence about him, and she really wanted us to pursue retaining him.

We parked right in front of his office on Cameron Street. I was impressed with the beautiful Victorian home and Old Town location. We arrived on time and walked up the front of the snowy steps together. I went to push the doorbell but before I could, the door opened. A slight five foot eight-inch-tall, African American man opened the door. He wore a pinstriped suit with a red tie and crisply pressed white shirt.

"Good morning, Mr. and Mrs. Sherrod," he said, "let me help you." He took my gloved hand and guided me up another couple of steps. Gene held my arm as I let him know how many steps we were encountering. We entered into the foyer and stepped onto a marble floor adorned with a small oriental rug. There were walls on both sides and ceramic tiles went halfway up to the ceiling. Memories flooded my mind of our house on Bryant Street which had a similar entrance. A small chandelier lit our path onto hardwood floors.

"Please come this way. I am glad to see you," Attorney Bynum said. "How was traffic?"

"It was light, thankfully," I said. "Perhaps due to the snow."

"Please let me take your coats," he responded.

He put our coats in the closet and we exchanged handshakes. The office, which maintained all the charm and beauty of old Victorian homes, was lovely. Attorney Bynum guided us to a conference room on the left, which looked like a law library. It was furnished with beautiful, rich, mahogany furniture and leather chairs. A fireplace with a nice painting was in the center of the room, and the chandelier was brass. I was impressed.

"Please take a seat, Mr. and Mrs. Sherrod. Would you like any coffee or water?"

Gene asked for coffee. I did not want to trouble him. If I needed to drink, I would take a sip of Gene's coffee. I put my purse in the upholstered chair next to me and took out my portfolio. It was time to get down to business.

Attorney Bynum smiled at us and said, "I already know a lot about you."

Gene and I exchanged a look as if to say, "How does he know so much about us?" I figured Attorney Bynum had conversed with Attorney McDaniel who handled our criminal case.

Attorney Bynum introduced himself, sharing personal information with us about his family, where he was from, and his career in Washington, DC. He went into detail about the criminal and civil cases that he had won and some of the well-known clients he represented. He shared in-depth about two cases he'd won involving police abuse of power and excessive force in civil court.

Feeling great about him, I was able to relax.

My anxiety level decreased, and I could tell my coursing blood pressure was down.

When he asked us to tell him about ourselves, another attorney entered the room.

"This is my partner, Attorney Jenkins," he said.

After more greetings and more handshakes, we told him about us. However, before we into too much detail I asked him, "What do you know about us?"

"Your criminal lawyer, Attorney McDaniel, informed me that 'you and Mr. Sherrod are 100 percent African Americans who are educated, Christians, worked all of your lives, upper-middle class and community oriented.' Attorney McDaniel is my frat brother," he continued. "I trust him and his judgment. He was emotional about your case and the injustice purported on you by the police officer and MPD. I am not sure if you are aware, Mr. and Mrs. Sherrod, but Detective McHugh trampled all over your constitutional rights. Attorney McDaniel and I watched the security video together. We spent about two hours reviewing it, taking notes, and making observations about every aspect from beginning to end. And to tell you the truth, I have never seen a situation like this before. You did not have a gun, the other driver was the aggressor, and there was even a witness walking back and forth in front of the flower shop. Detective McHugh did not have probable cause to pursue criminal charges. Based on the information that I have about your criminal case, and what I have learned about you and Mr. Sherrod's background, I would be happy to take this case and file a civil lawsuit on your behalf."

Gene smiled broadly, "That's great, Attorney Bynum."

I was relieved and grateful. We had finally found a lawyer to represent us.

We learned from Attorney Bynum that we did not have a lot of time to file the lawsuit, so he began work immediately. As we discussed the terms of hiring Attorney Bynum, we reflected on all the issues that led us to him. Analyzing the timeline of events, we realized the District had a strategy for keeping me in limbo from May 15, 2015 to January 2016. The District dropped the criminal case on January 6, 2016, almost to the day of the approaching deadline to bring a lawsuit against them. When I went before Judge Sullivan in August 2015 thinking the criminal charge would be thrown out, the judge realized the bull was already out of the gate, so he "kicked the can down the road" without taking time to watch the video. The judge's ruling of probable cause gave life to Detective McHugh's and the claimant's lies. Although the judge said he would like to "see her sit in a chair squirming and telling her lies," that was just a smoke screen. He had my life in his hands and could have put an end to it that day. Instead, the grand jury would get to hear the case and decide whether to indict me or not. Could the District's goal to prevent a civil lawsuit and deny our chance of pursuing justice for violation of our constitutional rights be the reason why my case dragged out so long from August

11, 2015, when Judge Sullivan remanded the case to the grand jury to settle?

Fortunately, God blessed us and gave us more time to invoke our friend, JUSTICE, and we had a great lawyer who believed in us and was willing to help.

After retaining Attorney Bynum, Gene, Ginger, Danton, and I decided to go on a family vacation. We rented a Cadillac Escalade and drove to Charlotte, North Carolina, for a stay at the Ballantyne Hotel, a high-end, luxury hotel in a beautiful, woodsy, green suburb. There was an eighteen-hole golf course, an Olympic size swimming pool, and well-appointed guest rooms on the property. It was the first time we'd been on vacation in a year. Being there was like a balm in Gilead.

We decided to stay an entire week so everyone could rest, relax, reflect, and renew. Even though I was still having difficulty sleeping and experiencing occasional triggers, it was the best I'd felt in quite some time. When I walked into the suite overlooking the golf course, I felt like I shed twenty pounds. "Gene, oh my goodness, this room is wonderful."

"Do you like it, darling?" he responded.

"Yes, I do."

The room was large with a California king-sized bed and stately appointed with oriental rugs, carpet, and wall coverings in blue, gold, beige and teal embroidery that created a serene atmosphere. Mahogany end tables sat next to large barrel chairs where I planned to spend a lot of time reading, watching television, praying, and meditating. Ginger scheduled spa appointments and other activities for us to enjoy during our stay. But that first evening, we put on evening attire and had a five-course dinner in the formal dining room.

By 5 p.m. we were dressed and ready to go downstairs. Gene looked handsome in his suit and laundered white shirt with cufflinks. I wore a blue and black silk dress. I did not think we were overdressed since the restaurant was formal. Even if we were, I didn't care. This was how we typically dressed when enjoying fine dining.

We met Danton and Ginger in the dining room, and they were formally dressed also. It's just how we do things in our family. We selected a table with a view and sat down to order cocktails and hors d'oeuvres.

"So, Mommy, what are we going to do tomorrow," Ginger asked.

"Well, I want to see family and go to York to check on the property."

"Makes sense, we need to see everyone while we are here for a week."

Once we planned out the next day and the rest of the week, we toasted in celebration. Finally, there was something to celebrate other than the grand jury throwing out the case and not indicting me. After dinner, we all hugged and walked to our respective rooms with plans to have breakfast at our favorite place in Clover, South Carolina the next morning.

(Ginger) Danton and I retired to our room and decided to watch a movie. While Danton selected the movie, I powered up my computer to check my emails. Since I had nothing new in my inbox, I checked Mommy's. There was an unread email from Kenneth Bynum with the subject line: "Complaint." I opened the email.

"Oh my God, I have to call Mommy! Hooray! Hooray! Yippee!"

It was late when the phone rang, and I picked it up after about three rings thinking it must be a wrong number. "Hello?" I answered tentatively.

"Mommy, it's me! Oh my God you are not going to believe this!"

"What?"

"Kenneth Bynum filed the complaint against the District, MPD and Simpson!" Ginger screamed.

"What is it?" I asked.

"$20 million dollars!"

Five minutes later Ginger was knocking hard and fast on our door. I raced to the door and opened it. Clad in her pajamas with her laptop in her arms, she jumped on our bed like a two-year-old before I had a chance to say anything.

"Mommy, Dada, I have to read this to you!"

Ginger read the entire complaint. Our lawsuit. Forty-three pages in total, and she read each count with a passion that I had never heard. On April 21, 2016, Brother Justice was on the horizon.

Count One – Violation of Vashti Sherrod's Fourth Amendment Rights – Searches, Seizures, Arrests Made Without Probable Cause

Count Two – Violation of Vashti Sherrod's Fourth Amendment Rights – Malicious Prosecution

Count Three – Violation of Eugene Sherrod's Fourth Amendment Rights – Searches, Seizures, Arrests Made Without Probable Cause

Count Four – False Arrest and False Imprisonment of Plaintiff Vashti Sherrod

Count Five – False Arrest and False Imprisonment of Plaintiff Eugene Sherrod

Count Six – Malicious Prosecution in Violation of the Common Law of the District of Columbia

Count Seven – Assault on Plaintiffs Vashti Sherrod and Eugene Sherrod

Count Eight – Negligence towards Plaintiffs Vashti Sherrod and Eugene Sherrod

Count Nine – Negligent Infliction of Emotional Distress on Plaintiffs Vashti Sherrod and Eugene Sherrod

Count Ten – Intentional Infliction of Emotional Distress on Plaintiffs Vashti Sherrod and Eugene Sherrod

Count Eleven – Detective McHugh and Simpson Liability for Punitive Damages

Count Twelve – District of Columbia False Arrest and False Imprisonment of Plaintiff Vashti Sherrod

Count Thirteen – District of Columbia Malicious Prosecution of Plaintiff Vashti Sherrod

Count Fourteen – District of Columbia Negligence Toward Plaintiff Vashti Sherrod

Count Fifteen – District of Columbia Negligent Infliction of Emotional Distress Plaintiff Vashti Sherrod

Count Sixteen – District of Columbia

Intentional Infliction of Emotional Distress Plaintiff Eugene Sherrod

Count Seventeen – Simpson's Negligence Toward Plaintiffs Vashti Sherrod and Eugene Sherrod

After reading the entire complaint, we all held hands— crying, praying, rejoicing, and celebrating until early in the morning.

Dear Justice, please come. Please come to us through our Lord and Savior Jesus Christ.

PART TWO

Welcome to the second part of *Reclamation: Breaking Chains of Racism and Police Brutality.* The book's opening chapter entitled 'Summer Flowers' begins with the simple act of buying flowers. On that day, my seventy-seven-year-old self encountered a white woman who met for the first time in her life a black Queen. One who would not grovel and succumb to her intimidations, threats, and lies. One who would call upon the deep reservoir of power in her soul to rest herself free of her grip. One who would use the legal system to snap the chains of racism and police brutality that attempted to dethrone her with a grip on her life.

My journey from this point in the book traverses the precipice of a mountain of legal entanglements and engagements used as stones and boulders to break down the wall of racism and the pit of hell that I was tossed into. How many of us have uttered the words "I will sue" to reclaim what was broken, stolen, and taken away? Rights. Simply, rights. Well, I did, we did. We sued.

From the moment we filed the complaint, the layers of lies from Ms. Simpson, Detective McHugh, and their lawyers intensified to suffocate our truth. The truth journey from beginning to end was the act of telling my story, over, and over again, which is the legal process. When you are innocent, the process of revealing truth from lies is what made me sick both physically and mentally. But with my truth, real facts were produced that demonstrated without a doubt that we should not have been in this predicament. There was evidence from the very beginning, irrefutable evidence, that showed the use of unscrupulous power to injure us. The revelation of facts layer by layer are revealed in the pages to follow.

It takes strength and courage to survive a lawsuit and the determination to fight until the bitter end of it. We would rather have had our time, our life, our freedom. But it was important to fight for all the Black women and men who cannot fight the 'Karen' of our time. Those who do not have resources and must stay quiet—who must go on with their lives carrying the pain of injustice in their soul.

In the Bible, when Paul and Silas were jailed and subsequently freed to go, Paul refused requesting the Roman officials come and let them out given that they were not found guilty. Paul sent back words to the officials that he was a Roman citizen who was unjustly punished and thrown into prison and that *he would not leave in secret.*

I am Vashti, daughter of Marion and Cazetta Sanders, descendants of Africans who survived the transatlantic passage, and of Native Catawba Indians who survived near extinction in America. I will not go quietly, and neither should any of us. Ever living in a state of reclamation.

CHAPTER 17

My Sworn Testimony and Deposition

The road to justice is slow, expensive, exhilarating, exhausting, exasperating, emotional, effervescent, and sometimes, evil. Our hardworking attorneys charted out a path that was clear, logical, and professional. They were passionate, going above and beyond every step of the way. They even met us at our home to keep us from driving to their offices.

After filing the complaint, we moved on to discovery, taking the sworn testimony and depositions of all defendants and plaintiffs. The District of Columbia represented Detective McHugh through an attorney, Simpson had her own attorney, and we, of course, had ours.

For me, the depositions were intense, emotional, terrifying, and yet freeing. My blood pressure, PTSD, gastrointestinal and other issues flared. Gene was emotional most of the time. We spent hours and hours and hours in small conference rooms with the defendants and attorneys coming within mere feet of us, including Simpson.

A long-time physician friend of mine told me that sometimes lawsuits were worse than what you were suing about. I felt like that occasionally, but most of the time I was reclaiming my power. My psychiatrist was a huge help as I was able to talk through my issues with her after each meeting. She helped me to prepare for my first deposition. I was so incredibly nervous, and I really don't know why. Perhaps because it was the first time I met and interacted with the District of Columbia government lawyers whose goal would be to defend the rights of the person who pursued Gene and I relentlessly. Dr. Richards gave me tools to hold onto in my mind in order to relax, stay focused and not get stressed. They all worked! I was in good form as I navigated through the questions they asked and traps that they set. Thankfully, I had appointments with Dr. Richards to talk about my experiences. I decided to drive alone to my next nine a.m. appointment. Dr. Richards was always on time, so I got there a bit early. As I opened the door she was standing there with a big smile on her face.

"Hi, Vashti, come on in. I just got here."

I stepped inside and took a seat in the usual place.

"It's cold out there," she said.

"Yes, it is," I responded. "Very."

"Well, how have you been?" she asked.

After our pleasantries, we got straight down to business. Remembering that I was deposed a few weeks ago by the District, Dr. Richards knew exactly where to pick back up from. And I shared with her what she wanted to know — the entire experience, every question, every word. It gave me great comfort to share it all with her. I started from the very beginning. The very first words:

"Good morning, Mrs. Sherrod. How are you?"

"I am well, sir."

"I think we introduced ourselves at the hearing for Mrs. Simpson some time ago. Just for the record, let me formally introduce myself and tell you what my role in this case is. I am David Jackson, an assistant attorney general, and I am representing Detective McHugh in this lawsuit. Okay?"

"Okay."

Without introducing himself, Attorney Bynum interjected. Attorney Jackson was not clear in his introduction and failed to state that he represented the District of Columbia.

"I am sorry." Attorney Jackson said. "I want to focus my questioning on your interaction with Detective McHugh, so I am going to pick up pretty much from that point. Okay? Now, it is my understanding that on May 16th of 2015, there was a card – a business card left at your home address by Detective McHugh. Is that correct?"

I stated yes.

"Okay. And was that the first time that you had had any information that there was a

Detective McHugh with the DC Police Department?"

Again, I stated yes.

"Between the accident on May 14th, and the time that you saw Detective McHugh's card at your address, his business card, were you aware that Mrs. Simpson had contacted the Metropolitan Police Department?"

"No, sir."

"Okay. Were you informed by your insurance company that Ms. Simpson had made any kind of claim arising out of the accident that you had on May 14th?"

"No, sir."

"So, is it fair to say from when you left the front of Ginkgo's flower shop on May 14th, the next time that you had any information relating at all to this accident was when you saw Detective McHugh's card, is that correct?"

"Yes, sir."

"How many times did you attempt to call Detective McHugh?"

"Two or three times."

"Okay. And when was the first time you tried to call him?"

"May 16th."

"That was the day that you saw the card – his business card at your address?"

"Yes, sir."

"And you were not able to get in touch with him, is that correct? Were you still at home – when I say home, I am referring to your home in Maryland on May 16th?"

"Yes."

"And when was the next time that you attempted to contact Detective McHugh?"

"In another day or two."

"Okay. And you were unsuccessful?"

"That is correct."

"Okay. And at that point did decide you knew why Detective McHugh had left his card at your residence?"

"No."

"At that point, had you put in a claim to your insurance company relating to the repairs of the damage to the mirror of your vehicle?"

"I called her insurance company, USAA."

"And did you talk to somebody?"

"Yes."

"Did any – did anyone from the USAA Insurance tell you that Ms. Simpson had made any kind of claims or made any statements relating to the accident that you had on May 14th?"

"No, sir."

"And when... I believe at some point, you did get in touch with Detective McHugh, is that correct?"

"Yes."

"Do you remember what day that was?"

"May 21st, there about."

"And were you still in Maryland when you talked to him?"

"Yes. Or I was leaving Maryland."

"Yes. Okay."

"So, when you say that you were leaving Maryland, what do you mean by that?"

"We were going to South Carolina. And when I called him, I believe I called from my cell phone because I really wanted to resolve it."

"So, when you were able to first talk to Detective McHugh, to the best that you can recall, I want you to walk me through that conversation. So, in other words, you dialed his number again, and at some point, he answered. And tell me about that conversation."

"He answered, and I identified myself. And he said... I told him that I had been trying to get in touch with him for several days now. He responded by saying that he was in training, that was how come he had not spoken with me. And then he said, 'I came out to your home to investigate an incident that happened at a garden shop where you – I think he used the word – you assaulted a lady with a gun. And I need to search your car. I could have searched it that day when I came out and put the card in the mail. I could have even seized your car. I could have arrested you then.'

"Then he went on to say... I said, well, I did not have a gun. I have never had a gun. I do not own a gun. And he said, 'you were caught on video and the video is downtown in the prosecution's office. Where is your car right now, I want to search your car?'

"And I said to him, my husband... my car will not be available, my husband and I are going to South Carolina. As a matter of fact, we are on our way because I have business to look after. And I told him, Detective McHugh, I will call you as soon as I return."

"Okay. So, when you first heard Detective McHugh's voice, can you describe his – the tone of voice, his tone of voice?"

"When he addressed the fact that he had been in training and that was why we were unable to talk, I felt okay. It was soft. But then, when he told me where I was and what I did and that I had a gun, I refuted that right then. I did not have a gun. I have never had a gun, and I do not own a gun."

"Okay."

"So, he got a little brash with me in the conversation. And when he told me, 'Oh, I could have seized your car then when I came to the mailbox and I could have searched it, and I could have arrested you,' then his conversation changed, and it was brash and intimidating to me."

"When you finished your conversation, what did you say to your husband?"

"I told him, 'now I realize... now I know why the card was placed in our mailbox and what this is all about.' And we discussed it."

"Okay. And tell me about that conversation."

"I repeated to him what Detective McHugh said to me because he could not hear it. So, I just told him our conversation. And that was that."

"So, tell me, on June 24th, what happened that led to you having some interaction with Detective McHugh?"

"We were in our car and we were riding on Capitol Hill. I believe that's Independence Avenue, Southeast near the Library of Congress and the Sam Rayburn Building, just about where First Street crosses in there. And I first casually heard something coming up on me. It could have been a siren, I thought. And

I looked in my rearview mirror. So, I pulled over and immediately stopped at the curb. I was almost at the intersection, so I just pulled over and I stopped. And I looked in my rearview mirror and there were two police officers pointing shotguns. They had them on the mirrors just like that. So, I am like, 'oh, my god, what is this?'

"And I was terrified. So, I ducked down, and I told my husband, I said slide down in your seat, we are going to get shot. So, I slid down as much as I could, holding onto my steering wheel. And he just took his head and bent it like that. And then, when I was down, one police officer came over to my window with his gun drawn and another one came up to my husband's window and drew his shotgun on him."

"How many police cars were there?"

"I did not... I do not know about the police cars. There were three police officers."

"Did the... did the police try to communicate to you by using their loudspeaker that may be on the police car?"

"No."

"Okay. So, when you first noticed that there were police behind you, were their lights and sirens going?"

"I saw the guns. I did not... I... I do not know."

"Okay. Let me make sure I am clear."

"Okay."

"You said at some point there were police behind you, and you pulled over to the curb. When you saw them behind you, were their lights flashing and the siren going? I mean, could you hear them before... did you hear them before you saw them?"

"I don't recall that."

"Okay. And so, once you pulled over, at that point, did you realize that they were stopping you?"

"Yes."

"How did you know that?"

"I saw the guns first. And I heard them telling me to pull over."

"How were they telling you to pull over?"

"I do not recall all that."

"Well, they were not at your car window telling you to pull over, correct?"

"They... there were two in the back window. There... There were two police officers with guns pointing at us in the... in the back window of the car."

"Were they in the—"

"There was another one, a third one, that came around to the driver's side and pointed at me. And then I looked to my right, there was another one pointing at my husband."

"So, what I am trying to understand, Mrs. Sherrod—"

"Yes?"

"Is as you are driving, at some point you realize there are police behind you, correct? Indicating... And when you realize that they are behind you, you look in your rearview mirror and you see twenty police cars, correct? Is that correct? Is that correct?"

"I saw... I saw the guns and the officers."

"Did you see—"

"That is what I remember."

"Okay. But did you see the guns and the officers before you saw the police car?"

"I saw the guns."

"Okay. And on the officers, you said, they approached your vehicle. Is that correct?"

"My side."

"Your side? You were driving?"

"And another one approached my husband's side."

"And the officer that approached your side, he had his gun in his hand?"

"Yes."

"Not a shotgun, but his service revolver?"

"No, it was a gun like that. A shotgun. He had a shotgun. Well, it is like what we called it in the country. I have not seen one of those in a while. It was like... about that like that. And...because... given the hands like maybe about twelve inches, fourteen inches? I do not know. It was long."

"Okay. And the officer that approached the driver's side, what did he have in his hands?"

"Same thing."

"The same type of gun?"

"Yes."

"The same length?"

"Yes."

"And what about the third officer, where was he?"

"The passenger."

"So, there were two on the passenger side and one on the... on your side, is that correct?"

"That is correct."

"Okay. And was your window, at that point, was your window up or down?"

"It was up initially. I put it down when he approached me, I put it down."

"And did he tell you to put it down or did you just put it down?"

"I put it down because he stood his shotgun beside him."

"Okay."

"He put his gun down."

"Okay. So, he put his gun down once he... once you rolled down your window, correct?"

"Once he held it to me like that."

"Right. And when, at some point, did he—"

"And then he put it down and I put the window down."

"Okay. And did you see what the other two officers on the passenger side did with their weapons?"

"I only looked out the right side of my face, and I saw a police officer on the other side of the car, the passenger side where my husband was sitting. And there was one officer there. I do not know what happened to the third one, but I know there were three."

"Okay. And the window, the passenger side window, was that up or down?"

"It was up. He never... I do not think he put his down."

"So, when you told your husband to slump down or get down in the seat, did you tell him why?"

"Yes. I was screaming."

"You were screaming?"

"Yes."

"And were you curious at all, or were you concerned at all, why are these officers approaching me in this manner?"

"I did not have time to think about that. I was thinking about my safety and if these guys were going to kill me."

"And what made you think that they were going to kill you?"

"The gun was pointed at my head."

"It could have been a mistake."

"It was on our heads."

"So, other than the guns being pointed at you, they did not say nor do anything that made you think that they were going to kill you, correct?"

"They did not have to."

"They did not have to? What did the officers say to you when they approached the car?"

"He said to me, 'Where have you been? This car has been reported. It was reported that this car was involved in criminal activity.'"

"And what did you say?"

"I answered his first question first."

"Where have you been?"

"Yes. And—"

"I am sorry, go ahead."

"I told him that we had just left Euro Motorcars in Bethesda, Maryland. And just to provide proof, I reached in my compartment and I showed him the paper. He glanced at it, where the car had been serviced that morning. And we had left there. And he looked at it and he gave it back to me and I put it down. I had a bottle of water. That was the next step. I said, 'see here is my water. Here is my water.' And he said, 'oh, your bottle has Euro Motorcars on it.'"

"Has what?"

"Euro Motorcars on it, the label on the bottle of water. And so, he said... his comment was, 'Well, I...' It was just, 'Well, I really do not know where Euro Motorcars is; I am not from this area.' I said it is where we have this car serviced. And he said, 'Well, I am not going to arrest you senior citizens.' And I stopped crying."

"And you stopped crying?"

"I stopped crying because he assured me, us, 'I am not going to arrest you senior citizens.'"

"So up until that point, you were crying?"

"Yes, sir."

"Okay."

"Then my husband grabbed the glove box and he pulled out the registration and the insurance card. It was all in a little package. And he gave him that. And I grabbed my, he handed me my wallet out of my purse, and I gave out my driver's license and my husband gave his... his ID.

"At this point they were nice to us. They told me to relax for a minute, that they, that he was going to go and make a phone call."

"That who was going to make a phone call?"

"He, the police officer."

"The police officer? At... Prior to the time that he said, 'I'm not going to arrest you,' and you said that you were crying, did you ever ask him why they had stopped you?"

"He told me."

"What did he tell you?"

"He said the car has been involved in criminal activity."

"Did you ask him what criminal activity the car was involved in?"

"I do not recall if I did at that point in time. I mean—"

"Well, wouldn't you want to know what they were talking about, that your car was involved in criminal activity?"

"I believe I could have asked him that, but he did not elaborate."

"I understand that. But—"

"Or I can't remember, you know, what he said. I believe I did ask him that question during all the stuff we were trying to do and pull together.

"First, I knew in my heart that the car had been with us the whole time and it was not involved in any criminal activity. So, I just felt whatever it was, we were going to have to work through this."

"Tell me, from the time that you pulled over to the curb until the time that the officer said, 'I am not going to arrest you senior citizens,' how much time had elapsed?"

"From what?"

"From the time that you pulled over to the curb until the time that the officer told you he was not going to arrest you, how much time had gone by?"

"Well, he said that almost in the beginning when he saw us."

"Okay. So, when he approached the car, after you rolled down the window, that is when he said he's not going to arrest you?"

"I do not recall the exact sequence. I can only say that I know he initially asked us where we had been."

"Okay."

"And then after that, he said, and he looked at us carefully, 'I am not going to arrest you senior citizens.'"

"Other than telling you that the car had been reported to have been involved in a crime, did the officer specifically tell you anything about the nature of the crime that he was referring to?"

"No, and no."

"At that point, did you think in your own mind, is this related to my conversation with Detective McHugh?"

"Objection to form," interjected Attorney Bynum.

"You can answer," the judge said.

"I did not think about it then."

"At some point during that or after the stop, did you see Detective McHugh?"

"Yes."

"How long after the stop did Detective McHugh appear on the scene?"

"Probably about a half an hour, forty minutes. We waited."

"At any time before Detective McHugh arrived on the scene did the police officers that stopped you, did they go back and sit in their police car?"

"Yes."

"Okay."

"Some of them. Some of them."

"Was there always a police officer standing next to your car between the time that they stopped you and the time that Detective McHugh arrived on the scene?"

"With my husband, yes."

"So, he was standing on the passenger side?"

"Yes."

"But not on your side, correct?"

"Yes."

"He was not standing on your side the entire time, correct?"

"No."

"Sometimes I am not sure, when I ask the question if the yes or no means, no that my questions was correct or no that what I am saying is correct?

"So, we are clear for the record at some point the officer who was standing on your side of the car left and went back and sat in his police car, correct?"

"Yes."

"But the officer that was on your husband's side stood there during that whole period?"

"Yes."

"I might have just asked you this. Do you remember from the time that the officer left your side of the car until the time that Detective McHugh showed up, how much time had elapsed?"

"It's hard... difficult for me to measure the time. Because—"

"Ma'am, don't guess. We don't want you to guess. Tell him what you know," the judge said.

"It's difficult for me to measure the time. So, he left, went to his car. He came back to tell us... maybe ten... ten minutes that it will not be too much time before someone comes. He didn't say the name. I said okay."

"You anticipated my next question. So, you had no idea that this someone that the officer was referring to was Detective McHugh?"

"No."

"Okay. And prior to Detective McHugh coming to your car, had you ever seen him before?"

"No."

"So, tell me what happened once Detective McHugh arrived on the scene.

"I am sorry, before you...did you, did he talk

to the other police officers before he talked to you? Do you know?"

"I do not recall that."

"Okay."

"So then tell me about Detective McHugh arriving on the scene and your interaction with him."

"He got us out of the car. And we walked around the—"

"Let me... I do not mean to cut you off. But when you said he got us out of the car, can you tell how he did that?"

"Well, we got out of the car to talk with him."

"He told you to get out of the car?"

"Yes."

"And both you and your husband got out of the car?"

"Yes. I believe so."

"Okay."

"All right. And we went to the back of the car. His car was behind us. And I saw him, he saw me. And he started like... he started laughing."

"Laughing?"

"Yes, sir. Laughing. He said, 'remember me?' And he continued to laugh. And he pulled out a piece of paper and he said, 'Mrs. Sherrod, you can sign this paper for me to search your car. If you do not sign this paper, I will seize your vehicle.' That is what he said."

"When he said, 'Do you...do you remember me,' what did you say to him?"

"Nothing. Because that was harassing me and laughing."

"So, am I understanding? So, am I understanding... Because you said that Detective McHugh's car was behind yours. So, there was some space in between your car and the police officer's vehicle that originally stopped you?"

"I did not see that anymore. They had left by this time. I did not see his car.

"But the officer was still there because he was holding up on my husband."

"Right."

"One stayed."

"So, when you say that Detective McHugh was laughing—"

"Yes, sir."

"Can you describe his laugh for me?"

"He... I was standing on the side. 'Ha ha ha, remember me, ha ha ha.' And I'm, huh?"

"And did you... You said nothing to him?"

"Nothing to him."

"You didn't say, 'I don't remember you?' or 'No,' you didn't say, 'no?'"

"I didn't feel safe."

"All right. And so, after he said, 'do you remember me,' what is the next thing you remember him saying?"

Like I said before, he showed me the paper about search warrant. I... 'You can sign this, and I can search your car. If you don't sign it, I will seize your car.'"

"Did he at that point tell you or identify himself to you?"

"Yes."

"Okay. So, he... that was at first and then he laughed. And this is what I'm, this is what I'm trying to do, Mrs. Sherrod. And I know, you know it's probably looking at it, the overall picture. I try to go step-by-step, word-by-word, just so I can get a clear vision of what's going on at the scene."

"Yes, sir."

"So, he does introduce himself or tells you, I am Detective McHugh or something to that effect, is that correct?"

"Yes."

"Okay. And this is as he... he has now gotten out of his car and approached you, correct?"

"Yes."

"And when he said, I am Detective McHugh, did you say anything to him?"

"No."

"Did you remind him of the conversation—

"No."

"—that the two of you had over the phone?"

"No, sir."

"And so, the next thing that he said after he identified himself, is that when he started to laugh?"

"'Remember me,' yes."

"Okay."

"And you said nothing?"

"Yes, sir."

"After he said, remember me, what is the next thing that he said or did?"

"He gave me the paper."

"Okay."

"And did you ask him, what this paper is?"

"I read it."

"Okay."

"And you understood it?"

"Yes."

"Okay."

"And after you read it, what is the next thing that happened?"

"I signed it."

"Okay."

"And Detective McHugh told you or asked you to sign it?"

"He told me what my alternative was. 'Either you sign for me to search or I take it, I seize it.'"

"And seize it, being your car?"

"Yes."

"Okay."

"And did you ask him what he was searching for?"

"He... yes."

"Okay."

"What...what did he tell you he was searching for?"

"The gun."

"And did you ask him what gun he was talking about?"

"No."

"Did you ask him, 'who said I had a gun?'"

"No."

"Did you remind of him of the conversation that you had with him over the phone?"

"No."

"Did he explain to you, or did he describe to you the make or type or size of the gun he was looking for?"

"No."

"What did you say to him when he said he was going to look for a gun?"

"Nothing."

"Nothing? Okay. And did he then proceed to search your vehicle?"

"Yes."

"Okay."

"So, at that point when he started to search your vehicle, have you now told me the substance, to the best that you can recall, all of the things that he said to you from the time he arrived on the scene until the time that he started to search your vehicle? Do you recall if there was any other conversation whatsoever?"

"There was none."

"Okay."

"Did he talk to your husband, do you know?"

"No."

"And so, he then stated to search your car, is that correct?"

"Yes."

"Tell me about the search that he did, where did he go first?"

"I believe he started up front, like where we were sitting."

"Was it the driver's side or the passenger side?"

"Well, he was in that area going in through the driver's side. And then he went into the back seat, all in there. And then he popped the trunk, and he went all through the stuff in the trunk."

"And during this search process, did he say anything to you? As he's searching the vehicle, did he say anything to you?"

"No."

"Did you say anything to him?"

"No."

"Did your husband say anything to him?"

"No. The police officer was just trying to – stayed – the Capitol Hill police was busy trying to console him and he was trying to console me. It was just a lot going on and all the people from lunch, they were all over us and trying to help us. You know..."

"And these are people that you know, or just people?"

"They were out from the Sam Rayburn Building, the Library of Congress. It was lunch time."

"Okay."

"But my question is, are these people that you know or were they just strangers?"

"No, I did not know any of those people."

"So how long did Detective McHugh take to search your vehicle?"

"Probably around close to an hour."

"Okay. Were the Capitol Police there, or at least one of them there, for the whole hour?"

"Yes, sir."

"And other than the car, did he search any of your personal belongings such as your purse or your coat or anything like that?"

"They were all in the car. And I didn't watch him closely."

"And after the search ended, tell me what happened next."

"Detective McHugh approached me, and he said, 'I would like for you all now to follow me to 1D, to my office.'"

"Okay."

"I told him, no, I am not going to your office unless my counsel is with me."

"Okay."

"Did he say anything in response to that?"

"Not a word. He left."

"Excuse me?"

"No."

"Okay. What happened next?"

"We went about our journey."

"I'm sorry. So, Detective McHugh has now left the scene?"

"Yes, sir."

"Okay. So, let me ask you this. Have you told me everything that transpired from the time Detective McHugh was...came on the scene to the time that he left, to the best of your recollection?"

"Yes, sir."

Between June 24th and July 7th, did you do anything to find out what crime you had allegedly committed?"

"Objection to form," our attorney said.

"You can answer if you know," the judge said.

"We began to investigate various counsel and...and going over some people that we, you know, knew in the past, and just really talking and trying to figure out between the two of us, and also my daughter and some other close people, whether we thought that... or how serious this was. So, we had made our minds up that we would start seeking advice, counsel."

"And who were you seeking advice or counsel from?"

"Well, it was just various people that, you know, we know as friends. It still wasn't a serious decision because when...each time we would talk, we said, you know, this is terrible. And we always relied in our hearts on two things. Although we discussed it. And we know a ton of lawyers; we know a ton of people. And so... and nobody, we ...you know, just talk about it, well, you know said I think you need to get yourself a lawyer. But then we always relied upon our innocence and the fact that we were blessed with a video."

"Okay. And as of July 7th, had you seen the video?"

"No."

So how do you know what was on the–"

"Wait a minute, let me see. We had not."

"Okay. So then how did you know what was on the video?"

"I didn't know. What one thing I did know was there was no gun on the video. So, no worries."

How did you know that the video that Detective M. had referred to was not a video of some other incident?"

"I wouldn't know that."

"Did you... did you talk to your pastor at all about these events?"

"Later."

"And for the purposes of these questions, I'm... I am only going up to July 7th, okay?"

"Okay."

"We were in bed in our nightclothes at around, I would say 8:45, with the television on, just casually going to sleep... trying to go to sleep."

"Was it still light out around that time or was it starting to get–"

"It was getting dark or beginning to. So, the doorbell rang. And I guess, and I said to my husband, I said, 'someone is at the door.' And he said, 'Oh yeah, yeah, somebody is at the door.' And I said, 'but we're not expecting anyone, are we?'"

"So, we just continued to watch TV. The doorbell rang again. And I said, 'The doorbell's still ringing.' And so, he said, 'Oh, maybe they have the wrong house.' And I was like, 'Okay.'"

"Did you know who it was at the doorbell?"

"I had no idea because nobody comes to see me unless they call first."

"What floor were you on when you first heard the doorbell?"

"I was upstairs in my master bedroom in the bed."

"Okay."

"Does the master bedroom have windows?"

"It does."

"Does the window look out into the front of the house?"

"Yes."

"Okay."

"Do the windows also look out...does it

have a set of windows that looks out to the side of the house?"

"Yes."

"What side of house, the left side? If I'm standing in front looking at your front door, would your windows look out to the left side of the house or the right side of the house?"

"Right, from the door."

"Okay. So, the doorbell rang the second time. You didn't look out the window to see who?"

"We... no... to answer your question."

"So, after it rang the second time, what happened next?"

"I said, 'Well, somebody is still ringing the doorbell.' So, we just kind of said, 'Well, maybe they have the wrong house.' Sometimes that happens."

"When you say they rang the doorbell, did they hit it once or did they keep—"

"I don't recall how many times they hit it."

"You don't recall? Okay. It wasn't a continuous buzz, is that correct?"

"They rang it two times that I'm aware of."

"Okay. So, after the second time, at some point you realized that the police were out there, correct?"

"When they knocked the door down."

"Prior to that, you didn't know that the police were out there?"

"I did not know that."

"You never looked out your window?"

"We had... No, to answer your question."

"Did the police ever call your house?"

"I never heard a phone ring, plus there is no phone in my bedroom."

"Do you know if your cell phone was on silent or was it on...I guess it was non-silent, so that you could hear it when it rings?"

"I charge it at night in another room, generally."

"So how long after the second ringing of the doorbell were you aware that the police were outside your house?"

"When they broke down the door down."

"Okay. And how long... how much time had elapsed between the last time that they rang the doorbell and the time that they broke the door down?"

"Probably a half an hour. Because they hit on the backdoor, went around and hit on the backdoor. And that's when I thought... I said, "You know what, this is another home invasion.' And I started, I asked him, 'Where can I hide? What can I hide and what can I do? And I punched the alarm, and the alarm wouldn't go off. Just inside my bedroom, there's a pad on the wall."

"Do you house...does your house have an alarm, an alarm?"

"It does."

"Okay."

"And was your alarm on at the time that you heard the doorbells ringing, the doorbell ring... ringing? I'm sorry."

"I don't recall that. But I remember trying to engage it and I couldn't engage it. And I didn't understand why, so I thought it was a home invasion."

"Okay. I guess I misunderstood you. There's only one alarm system to your house, there's not an alarm system for your house and one for the bedroom, correct? It's for the whole house."

"It's for the whole house."

"So, you control it from your bedroom?"

"Yes, sir."

"Okay. And so that's why you were trying to activate the alarm for your house? After they hit on the backdoor. At any time before they... when you say they hit on the backdoor, what do you mean by hit?"

"Knocked hard... hard."

"So, let me make sure I understand this. You heard somebody ringing your bell twice. You heard somebody knocking at your backdoor, and at no time did you look out the window to see who that may have been?"

"Absolutely not."

"And you never heard your phone ringing, is that correct?"

"Never."

"Was the TV up loud?"

"Kind of, sort of."

"Was it... knowing your phone and how

loud it rings and knowing how high up or how loud the TV was, if your phone had rung, would you have been able to hear your phone over the TV?"

"Objection, speculation," Attorney Bynum said.

"You can answer if you can, ma'am."

"The... Normally I would be able, I guess, to hear the phone. I never heard the phone ring."

"Okay."

"Objection. Move to strike the last answer based on guessing," Attorney Bynum said.

"You may proceed."

"Who was in your house currently?"

"My husband."

"Anybody else?"

"No, sir."

"At any time prior to them hitting the door, did you hear anybody yelling outside your house that the police, 'We're the police, we're the police.' Did you hear anything like that?"

"I did not."

"When you heard them knocking at the backdoor and you said to yourself – or maybe you said to your husband, that this is another home invasion, did you go to get your phone?"

"I couldn't."

"Why couldn't you?"

"Because of the way the house is designed."

"Okay. So, explain to me why, given your location, I believe you said you were in the bedroom, and the location of wherever your phone was, why could you not get your phone?"

"The way the house is designed, walking out of my master bedroom, there are stairs from the hallway going down, then there's a foyer and then there's glass right there. That is not shielded, okay. If I had walked... this was my thought. If with all of that, if I had walked, and the other bedrooms are down there, away from the master bedroom. Had I walked down that hallway like this, the hallway's like that, the stairs are here, the front door is here, and all of this is open. Had I walked down the hallway and gone into any of those other rooms, whoever was on the porch, whom I did not know, or who was in the yard, and I was in a skimpy nightgown, plus I was scared, they could have seen me visually walking through the house. So, I wasn't going to go back there."

"You only had one cell phone?"

"We both have cell phones, but we normally turn them off at night. And we have the landline phone, which is not in my bedroom."

"Where is the landline phone located in relation to your master bedroom?"

"That's in my husband's study."

"Where is your husband's study located in relation to your master bedroom?"

"It's down the hallway, and you're going in the door from the master bedroom."

"On the same level?"

"Yes."

"Okay."

"Did you try to go, or did you think to go and pick up your landline and call the police to find out—"

"They would see me."

"So, they would have seen you from the second... I'm sorry. Your master bedroom is on the second level?"

"Yes."

"And they would have seen you from the second level and the lower level? You said that you walked downstairs and there's a foyer—"

"No, they could see me from the hallway from my bedroom."

"Where was your husband's cell phone?"

"Probably plugged up somewhere. I don't know."

"Could you have... would you have been able to get access to your husband's cell phone?"

"It was in his study."

"I thought... and that's where your landline was too, correct? In there. So, after you heard the knock on your backdoor, by the way, is that a glass door or is it a solid... solid, some other kind of material for the door?"

"Glass."

"Glass? Okay. And is there a screen door in between, an outside screen door for your backdoor?"

"No."

"Is it a full glass door?"

"Yes."

"And is that on the first level or the second level?"

"Second."

"And that opens into a porch or–"

"Deck."

"– or a deck. Okay. And are there stairs leading from the yard to the deck?"

"Yes."

"So, once you... after you heard the knocking on your backdoor, did you also hear any knocking on the front door?"

"No."

"So, what happened next after you heard the knock on the backdoor?"

"With me, what I did?"

"No, just in terms of the sequence of events. You heard a knock on the backdoor."

"What... I... when they knocked on the backdoor, I told my husband that it could be another home invasion or someone trying to break in because they went to the backdoor. Then after that, I... I told him, well, why don't you get up out of the bed. I was already out; I was sitting out of the bed. Because maybe we should hide; I wanted to go in my big closet and hide. I made suggestions to him. I said, 'this is serious, somebody is breaking in here.' And he was really kind of like stubborn about it. He was not moving or trying to get into the closet. And I was urging him. I said what do we do now. I asked him if we could push the windows on the front up. He said, well, if we are going to do something, we would use the back windows, right? I said, do they push up, are they painted shut."

"Are they what shut?"

"We had a conversation."

"I am sorry. You said are they something shut? Are they painted shut? Painted?"

"Yeah."

"Okay."

"Because we don't raise those windows over there, windows over there. So, we just... I was just really scared."

"So, when you asked—"

"And I looked in my closet. And when I pulled the closet open, it is a great big closet.

But that closet had a window it in and I looked at the window and I went, oops, I can't hide in here because it's a big window. They can see in a little, you know. So, we... I just crawled back in the bed. I didn't know what to do.

"We heard something go boom in the front door. I said, 'oh, my God, they're breaking in, somebody's breaking, I told you it was a home invasion.' And then they were like, 'police, police, come down.' And I'm like... I told him, 'Oh, it is the police.' We thought it was... I thought, oh, my God, they're breaking in the house, they're breaking in. And then the police say, 'Police, police, come down, put your hands on your head.' And we–"

"Did you hear them say police immediately after you heard the, the door being breached?"

"I heard the door and I said, 'Oh, my God, somebody's breaking. Police, police, police.'"

"Okay."

"By that time, they were, I guess, inside the house. Because when we came out, they were in front of the door with their guns drawn and told me to put my hands on top of my head. I obeyed that. And they took my husband and they handcuffed him."

"And what about you? What did they do to you?"

"No, they didn't do me. They just did him."

"Okay."

"But I had my hands over top of my head."

"Okay. And you came down from your master bedroom?"

"Yes, with my hands over my head."

"Okay."

"And... And... and I... and he went in front of me. And then they–"

"I'm sorry. He being?"

"My husband. He was in front of me."

"Okay. So, let me ask you a question."

"Yeah."

"I assume that your husband knows pretty much the layout of the house, correct?"

"He does."

"Okay."

"So, he does not need... does he need assistance from you or anybody else to come from the upper-level floor to a lower-level floor?"

"He always knows how to do that, and he holds onto the stairwell when he goes on down."

"Okay."

"So, on this evening, I don't know whether he holds on or not. I had my hands on my head. I was looking at all the police officers that were all over the foyer."

"But you know that you did not have to help him down the stairs, correct?"

"He got down... he got down the steps."

"So, you get down to the... this is the first level?"

"Yes."

"Okay. And what do you see?"

"I see police officers. Initially, when I looked at them, they had their pistols drawn. And he went down first, and they cuffed him. And I kept my hands on my head. And then I came down and I saw Detective McHugh standing to my left by my dining room. Then they...but I didn't know the other police officers."

"So, there were others?"

"And they took him and put him first... no.

They released his cuffs when they put him on the sofa in the living room."

"Where were you at this point?"

"I was walking behind him. And I sat beside him."

"And the room that you were in where your husband was seated in the–"

"On the sofa in the living room."

"In the living room. Was Detective McHugh in that living room?"

"He was standing in the foyer. And when... oh, when he came down and I saw him, I looked at him and I recognized him. And he goes, 'Remember me?'"

"He said that again to you?"

"He said it two times."

"Said it again. And the two times is when he said it at the time you were stopped?"

"Yes."

"And now that he's at your house?"

"In my house."

"Okay. When you saw Detective McHugh standing in your foyer, what thoughts went through your mind?"

"Objection, speculation," Attorney Bynum said.

"You can answer."

"Now that's speculating," Attorney Jackson said.

"I'm asking her what thoughts went through her mind. None of us want her to guess."

"You can answer, ma'am," Attorney Bynum said again.

"I can't recall all the thoughts I was...that ran over my mind."

"And you say that you recognized Detective McHugh because of the encounter you had at the time that you were stopped, is that correct?"

"Yes."

"Okay. Now at some point, did you have a conversation with Detective McHugh?"

"At my home?"

"Yes."

"Well, another police officer asked the question, do you all have a gun in this... No, they said, 'where is the gun.' And we immediately said, 'we don't have a gun.' And then I said, 'if there is a, if you find a gun in this house,' and I looked at Detective McHugh, 'someone put it there.'"

"Do you know what police force the officers who were in your house, the ones that first broke down your door, do you know what police force they were from?"

"I assume from just information that I have reviewed, that they were probably Bowie police or somebody. But at the time that the incident happened, I didn't know who they were."

"You didn't have any understanding of what police department they were from?"

"They were just police officers."

"When you saw Detective McHugh, you knew what police department he was from, correct?"

"Yes, I did."

"Do you know if there was anybody else there from the Metropolitan Police Department?"

"I don't know."

"Did any individual introduce themselves as Detective McHugh's supervisor?"

"No."

"So, did you have any conversation with Detective McHugh at your house?"

"No."

"Did he say anything to you?"

"No. Other than, 'Remember me.'"

"Right. And so, the... the officer that said to you, do you have a gun in this house was not Detective McHugh, is that correct?"

"Yes."

"Did you see what, if anything, Detective McHugh may have done while he was in your home?"

"Yes."

"What did you see him do?"

"Ransack my house."

"What did Detective McHugh do?"

"We were detained the whole time in the living room. We were not allowed to move around."

"Okay."

"So, his...one of his police officers who

went... who talked to me the whole time, she stayed in the living room with me, more or less, and looking around in the house, making conversation with me, coming back and forth."

"Do you know her name?"

"I'm not sure. But it could have been–"

"Don't guess," Attorney Bynum interjected. "Tell him what you know."

"But she stayed with you throughout this whole ordeal?"

"Yeah. And there was another police officer who started out, I guess... I'm not supposed to guess, who was not there, but came back and sat in the living room for a long time."

"So, let's get back to my original question. What did Detective McHugh do while he was in your house?"

"The female police officer was unhappy with the way that I looked in my living room with a little skimpy nightgown on. So, she said to me, Mrs. Sherrod, I am going to go to your bedroom and find you a robe or something to put on and I'll bring it back. I said, fine. She went up, she came back. She said, 'I really,' and she didn't bring anything. She said, 'I couldn't get any clothes because the detective is in your closet and master bedroom. But you're fine.'"

"Do you know if there were any detectives there from the Bowie Police Department?"

"Not with certainty."

"You're not...you're not sure?"

"I did not know any of them."

"So, when the female officer said to you, the detective is in your room, did she give you his name?"

"Yes."

"And what did she say?"

"She said, Detective McHugh is in your closet and bedroom and I cannot get you any clothes now."

"Okay. And what else did she say?"

"That was it."

"So, then my question, my original question is, what did he do. You said that he ransacked your home. What did he do to ransack your home?"

"In the closet, all my clothes were pulled

down off the racks. More importantly, all of my designer church hats were thrown down, straw, felt, all kinds of things. And they were all in the closet on top in boxes. And they were labeled what they are, so when I go to get one, I know what I'm getting dressed. And they were all like on the floor and trampled over. I mean, it was just in disarray. And my master bedroom, all the drawers were out, the clothes were down, and... Is that enough?"

"Did...do you know how many police officers went into your bedroom?"

"Well, seemingly... well, they finished at the same time and... that's the only one I know about. And that's because I was told."

Okay."

"But the female officer, from what you just said, she just told you that he was in your bedroom correct?"

"That's what she said, yea."

"And am I correct that she did not tell you that he took any of your clothes out of the closet, correct?"

"Correct."

"And she did not tell you that he emptied out or looked into any of your hat boxes, correct?"

"Correct."

And she did not tell you that he investigated any of your... the drawers in your dresser or your nightstand or anything like that, correct?"

"Correct."

"How long did the search last?"

"Wow. Approximately two hours or more."

"And for that entire two hours or more, other than Detective McHugh saying to you when you first saw him standing in the foyer, do you remember me, he said nothing else to you during that total two hours or more that he was there?"

"One more thing."

"Uh-huh?"

"The search is on."

"When did he say that?"

"When I was asked where the gun was, get the gun, or something like that. Where is your gun, let us know where it is, something to that effect. And then he responded, the search is on."

CHAPTER 18

The Expert's Opinion

Attorney Bynum came to our house for his weekly status update. He was always prepared and brought his associate with him. We always had lunch catered so that we could work a few hours and not worry about eating. So much effort had been put into the case including getting experts to opine and analyze the police practice and operations according to regulations, rules and laws governing their actions and the rights of citizens. We had the opportunity to review much of the material along with Attorney Bynum who would explain the analysis and answer our questions.

"Mr. and Mrs. Sherrod, here is a copy of the expert's opinion," he said. "Please read it, and I will enjoy this beautiful lunch that you have prepared for us! Thank you!"

Gene and I got close together and reviewed

it line by line. It was clear and concise, so we didn't have any questions. It started with:

It is important that patrol officers and first-line supervisors have a broad understanding of the criminal investigation process in order to ensure that they take those measures and avoid missteps that will better ensure the overall success of criminal investigations. Officer Patel of the First District was the officer who responded to the Metropolitan Police Department (MPD) dispatcher's request for assistance following Ms. Simpson's 911 call. Officer Patel interviewed Ms. Simpson about the incident. He had been trained at the MPD's police academy regarding the information that should be gathered to complete a report for the MPD. He took notes during the investigation and then returned to his vehicle and wrote his report. In deposition, Officer Patel testified that he had initially intended to classify the reported offense as an "assault with a dangerous weapon" (ADW), a felony.

Officer Patel discussed with his supervisor, Sergeant Architzeo, the specifics of his conversation with Ms. Simpson, including information about Mrs. Sherrod allegedly pulling a gun on Ms. Simpson. Sergeant Architzeo directed Officer Patel to classify the alleged crime as "threat to do bodily harm," a misdemeanor, which is reflected in the police report that Officer Patel prepared. The following day Detective McHugh, who was completing a one-year probationary period as a detective, was assigned to the case in order to conduct a follow-up investigation.

Officer Patel told Detective McHugh that his supervisor, Sergeant Architzeo, had previously directed him not to classify this incident as an ADW, but rather as "threats to do bodily harm," a misdemeanor. Without any additional information, Detective McHugh requested Officer Patel reclassify Mrs. Sherrod's' alleged criminal offense as a felony, ADW.

Officer Patel was in violation of the International Association Chiefs of Police (IACP) criminal investigation standard and his department's policies when he reclassified the event between Ms. Simpson and Mrs. Sherrod from a misdemeanor, "threat to do bodily harm" to a felony, "assault with a dangerous weapon" without having any additional evidence and in total disregard of what his superior advised him to do.

Detective McHugh appears to have requested a fellow police officer change his report to a felony instead of a misdemeanor in order to accommodate what appears to be his biases. The IACP Criminal Investigation Concepts and Issues Paper states "[t]he primary goal of the follow-up investigation is to gather information and evidence.... when the investigator reinterviews the victim and witnesses, he or she must test and retest the validity of their statements.... the investigator must be able to recognize that factors of fear, stress, relationship, friendship, or dishonesty color and affect the credibility of the responses.... All information gathered should be categorized as investigative leads rather than positive evidence of a suspect's guilt or innocence." It is inappropriate and unacceptable under the standards set forth by the IACP to introduce biases into the investigation as Detective McHugh did. The investigation should be fact-driven, and the investigation should follow the leads developed and information gathered. Moreover, the IACP Model Policy for Criminal Investigations provides that an investigative officer in charge of a follow-up investigation should "search for new witnesses; complete background checks on witnesses, victims, and suspects, as appropriate; and seek additional information from other officers."

Detective McHugh failed to conduct a proper investigation as described in both the IACP policy for criminal investigations and his department's policies and procedures. He failed to adhere to this and other IACP standards, in the following ways: Detective McHugh did not seek additional information from Sergeant Architzeo, a senior officer who had reviewed the evidence from Officer Patel's initial interview of Ms. Simpson and determined that the case should properly be investigated as a misdemeanor charge rather than a felony ADW charge.

While Detective McHugh obtained the video surveillance recording of the May 14, 2015 incident, he failed to realize that the video not only failed to corroborate Ms. Simpson's retelling of the events to Detective McHugh in his interview of her, the videotape contradicted her story. *In his written descriptions of the video recording, Detective McHugh repeatedly significantly misstated the events depicted in the video.* For example, Mrs. Sherrod is not shown to be bending over into her vehicle just prior to pointing her arm at Ms. Simpson. In fact, she is shown to be bending over at the driver's side of her car approximately forty-five seconds prior to the time she points her arm toward Ms. Simpson. Also, Ms. Simpson does not get into her car and leave immediately after Mrs. Sherrod pointed her arm at her but delays leaving for twenty-one seconds. Moreover, during that period, Mrs. Sherrod appears to continue to talk to Ms. Simpson through the latter's passenger window.

Worse yet, while Detective McHugh admitted that the video was not clear enough to see if Mrs. Sherrod had a gun in her hand, he nevertheless falsely stated in his subsequent affidavits that he prepared to obtain a search warrant for the Sherrods' home and to arrest Mrs. Sherrod and that the video actually "corroborated" Ms. Simpson's story that Mrs. Sherrod had pointed a gun at Ms. Simpson during the May 14, 2015 incident. In deposition, Detective McHugh claimed the video was too grainy to see what Mrs. Sherrod was holding in her hand but that "the video is clear enough to see movements, an arm outstretched in front of a person's body" and that "[t]o anyone in law enforcement, that's an indication of someone pointing a gun at somebody else." While the manner in which a person is holding their arm may be an indication that they are pointing something, it certainly does not establish that the person had a gun in her hand.

No reasonable officer would have come to the conclusion that Mrs. Sherrod was pointing a weapon simply by seeing the way she was holding her arm without any objective new information to support this conclusion. By submitting false affidavits to obtain search and arrest warrants, Detective McHugh violated the IACP national standards for obtaining search and arrest warrants, as well as his own department's policies and procedures governing warrant applications. The IACP defines probable cause to affect an arrest as "when facts and circumstances within an officer's knowledge are sufficient to warrant a prudent person, or one of reasonable caution, to believe that the suspect has committed, is committing, or is about to commit an offense."

Detective McHugh never had probable cause at any point in his investigation to pursue a criminal case against Mrs. Sherrod and no objectively reasonable police officer would have believed that probable cause existed under the facts of this case. By violating the search warrant standards, Detective McHugh violated the Sherrods' Fourth Amendment rights and placed the Sherrods at risk of being seriously injured or killed if they had not acted properly when the police entered their home. The police broke down the door of their home and entered with guns drawn, not knowing into what circumstances they were entering. An entry team must be highly alert to any suspicious movement when making an entry. If the Sherrods had quickly exited their bedroom and surprised the police officers, it would have been an extremely dangerous situation for the Sherrods in which they could have been shot and killed.

The video recording of the May 14, 2015 incident and its resolution is sufficient to enable me to see that when she raised her right arm, Mrs. Sherrod was merely pointing her hand and may have been holding a notepad in her right hand and not a gun. Detective McHugh contacted Detective Simmons of the City of Bowie Police Department and requested that she file an application in the Circuit Court for Prince George's County, Maryland for a search warrant of the Sherrods' home. He provided her with a draft search warrant application. Detective Simmons relied entirely on the information supplied to her by Detective McHugh and did not independently view the video recording. This, in effect, made the application for the search warrant entirely that of Detective McHugh.

These false statements contained in the application are a gross violation of his department's policies and procedures and the search warrant standard set forth by the IACP. Because he lacked probable cause to arrest Mrs. Sherrod, Detective McHugh violated IACP's arrest warrant standard and Mrs. Sherrods' Fourth Amendment rights. Detective McHugh's negligence and misconduct caused Mrs. Sherrod to needlessly undergo the embarrassing, humiliating, and frightening process of being arrested, handcuffed, booked, photographed, transported to the Superior Court of the District of Columbia for processing, and jailed.

Detective McHugh did not thoroughly vet and investigate Ms. Simpson, the alleged victim, to properly judge her credibility and any underlying ulterior motives that may have led her to file a report of this incident to the MPD long after the incident had concluded. It is inappropriate and grossly negligent to take the word of only one person, especially when dealing with an alleged violent crime. Moreover, after viewing the surveillance video of the May 14, 2015 incident, any objectively reasonable police officer would have re-interviewed Ms. Simpson and confronted her with the obvious inconsistencies between her story about what occurred during the incident (discussed above) and the starkly contrary video evidence. Detective McHugh violated the IACP criminal investigation standard by failing to do so.

In deposition, Ms. Simpson made the astonishing admission that she never saw a gun in Mrs. Sherrod's hand at any time during the May 14, 2015 incident. Had Detective McHugh interrogated Ms. Simpson properly during his May 15, 2015 interview of her, he would have discovered this fundamental flaw in Ms. Simpson's story that would have stopped his investigation in its tracks. Several months later, at the time of the grand jury, Detective McHugh discovered that Ms. Simpson had mental health issues and her credibility was undermined by the fact she changed her version of the weapon that she allegedly saw Mrs. Sherrod point at her. In deposition, Detective McHugh testified he uses social media in his investigations, but he never looked at Ms. Simpson's social media at any time during the investigation. Had he reviewed Ms. Simpson's Twitter postings at the outset of his investigation or anytime thereafter, he would have discovered Ms. Simpson's longstanding mental illness (bipolar depression) that predated the May 14, 2015 incident. Detective McHugh violated the IACP criminal investigation standard by failing to do so. The knowledge of Ms. Simpson's mental illness would have led any objectively reasonable law enforcement officer to question the veracity of Ms. Simpson's statements, especially given her long delay in reporting the alleged criminal conduct to law enforcement. Detective McHugh also failed to conduct a search to locate or interview an eyewitness to the incident in violation of the IACP criminal investigation standard.

, an employee of Gingko Gardens, was plainly visible in the surveillance video that was obtained and reviewed by Detective McHugh. If Detective McHugh had interviewed , he would have heard the witness's version of what happened. A gun was never seen by this witness, who was within a few feet of the incident when it occurred.

Detective McHugh placed information into the Washington Area Law Enforcement System (WALES) and the National Crime Information Center (NCIC) system for a felony lookout. He stated: "[i]f the vehicle is located, hold all occupants and seize the vehicle as evidence. Vehicle has been involved in an ADW offense."

In the alert's summary section Detective McHugh stated: "[a] suspect occupying the vehicle brandished a firearm at the victim while exchanging information following a traffic accident." However, Detective McHugh's statements had not been substantiated by his investigation. Moreover, Detective McHugh's alert made the car Mrs. Sherrod was driving a high-risk stop for any law enforcement officer who stopped the car. Therefore, any law enforcement officers who stopped the Sherrods' car would have approached it with guns drawn, as in fact occurred when the Capitol Police stopped the Sherrods' car. During the traffic stop, one mistake by the Sherrods or a miscalculation by one of the officers could have resulted in the officers discharging their weapons at the Sherrods. Detective McHugh put the Sherrods' lives in danger without good cause. It appears that he had a total disregard for the people he was sworn to protect.

Detective McHugh testified that the police department has its way of determining what investigation is needed to prosecute a case. However, in the criminal justice system in the United States, the police do not prosecute a case; it is the prosecutor's office who brings the case to the court system and, therefore, will be the ones to determine if the evidence is enough to prosecute a case.

Detective McHugh was grossly negligent in the way he pursued the investigation and worked outside the parameter of the standards set forth by the IACP in how a case should be investigated. After hearing the testimony of Ms. Simpson and Detective McHugh, the grand jury refused to indict Mrs. Sherrod, and on January 6, 2016, the ADW charge was dismissed by the U.S. Attorney's Office.

Mrs. Sherrod had to go through twenty long and painful months of investigation because of Detective McHugh's gross negligence in the performance of his duty and incompetence in how to run a simple investigation. Conclusion: It is my opinion, which I hold to a reasonable degree of professional certainty, that the incident that occurred between Ms. Simpson and Mrs. Sherrod was not investigated according to the national standards set forth by the IACP and Detective McHugh's own police department. It is also my opinion that if Detective McHugh had followed the proper protocol for criminal investigations, he would have developed information that would have quickly led to the investigation's termination and the dismissal of the charges against Mrs. Sherrod. If he had followed these standards, Detective McHugh would have discovered that Mrs. Simpson's versions of the events were incorrect and uncorroborated and that there was no reasonable basis to believe that Mrs. Sherrod had committed a felony or misdemeanor.

It is my opinion, which I hold to a reasonable degree of professional certainty, that:

(1) the criminal investigation performed by Detective McHugh was flawed and fell below the standard of care set by the IACP;

(2) Detective McHugh failed to determine any level of probable cause to conduct a felony investigation of Mrs. Sherrod for an assault with a dangerous weapon;

(3) no objectively reasonable police officer would believe that the actions Detective McHugh took during his follow-up investiga-

tion of the May 14,2015 incident were appropriate under the circumstances;

(4) Detective McHugh's actions were contrary to national police standards for probable cause in determining justification for a search warrant for the Sherrods' residence and the arrest of Mrs. Sherrod;

(5) Detective McHugh, in his reports and actions during his follow-up investigation, submitted police reports that were misleading, contained false information, and took actions that were contrary to national police standards for such activities, no objectively reasonable police officer would believe this to be proper; and

(6) Detective McHugh, in continuing to attempt to prosecute Mrs. Sherrod, despite the information obtained during his follow-up investigation, acted contrary to national police standards, and no objectively reasonable officer would believe this to be proper.

My opinions on my background and experience as a law enforcement officer with over twenty-six years of experience and as a police trainer with over thirty-five years of experience teaching and developing policies and procedures for conducting arrest techniques, including: making arrests, handling subjects, and preparation for arrest and search warrants.

Submitted by,

CHAPTER 19

THE DETECTIVE'S SWORN

Testimony and Deposition
Background & Preliminary Information

Deponent stated that his full name is Phillip McHugh, and he was [redacted]. Deponent is currently employed as a detective with the DC Metropolitan Police Department.

Deponent testified that he has testified under oath before in both the DC Superior Court and the U.S. District Court for the District of Columbia in connection with his work as a police officer but has never before personally been sued or sued someone else.

Deponent stated that he has been employed by the MPD since 2007. Since that time, he has had disciplinary action taken against him one time for an unauthorized vehicle pursuit.

Deponent stated that he believes that this occurred in 2012 or 2013 and that the department took one day of vacation from him (administratively) in lieu of a formal suspension. He was represented by a union representative in connection with that incident but not an attorney.

INTERACTION WITH D. SIMPSON

Deponent testified that he had never met or heard of D. Simpson before May 14, 2015.

Deponent testified that he first became aware that Simpson had a history of mental illness at a witness conference months after the arrest had been made. Deponent testified that while he was sitting in the prosecutor's office with Simpson and Ms. Walters, the prosecutor, Simpson told him that she had issues with her memory and that she took medicine for health issues.

Deponent testified that he did not look at Simpson's Facebook account at any time during the investigation, was not aware of whether she had one, and had never looked for her Facebook account. Deponent testified that he looked to see whether Simpson had a Twitter account after meeting with her the day of the witness conference and did not have difficulty finding her account. Deponent stated that he did not learn anything from Twitter other than that Simpson had an account. Deponent testified that he went back to look at whether Simpson had posted on the date of the May 14, 2015 incident but does not believe that she did.

Deponent testified that he first interviewed Simpson on May 15th at her home after he called her and asked if he could come over to speak with her. Deponent confirmed that the First District is less than a mile from Simpson's home. Deponent testified that during the interview deponent asked Simpson generally what happened, and she recounted the following:

Simpson told the deponent about how her service dog had died, that she had a service dog for a long time, and that she had just picked its ashes up from a place in Virginia and was stopping at Gingko flower shop to buy flowers to bury with the ashes. Simpson then told the deponent that while she was attempting to parallel park in front of the flower shop, she hit the side view mirror of a black Mercedes that was parked there. Deponent testified that Simpson specifically told him that the Mercedes was parked. Simpson then got out of her car to inspect the damage and exchange information with the other driver. Simpson stated that the other driver got out of the vehicle and began shouting and screaming at her while Simpson was attempting to fix the mirror of the Mercedes. Simpson said that Mrs. Sherrod refused to give her any information except her insurance card even though Simpson gave Mrs. Sherrod her license, registration, and vehicle insurance. Simpson stated that the parties argued for fifteen to twenty minutes and exchanged disparaging comments. Simpson claimed that she had suggested calling the police to sort everything out but did not believe that the police needed to be involved for such a minor accident. Simpson stated that somehow, she brought up the fact that her dog was dead and that she was having issues with her husband leaving and that Mrs. Sherrod used this information to insult her. Simpson told deponent that she responded that her ex-husband was Black but only liked white women and wouldn't want to be with Mrs. Sherrod. Simpson then stated that Mrs. Sherrod told Simpson that her insurance card was expired and asked her to call her insurance company and have a new card e-mailed to her, which Simpson told the deponent that she did. Simpson stated that she told Mrs. Sherrod that she was going to call the police since Mrs. Sherrod would not exchange information and went to the front windshield of the Mercedes to write down the VIN number of the vehicle. Simpson alleged that at this point she again asked Mrs. Sherrod for her license and Mrs. Sherrod responded, "I'm not going to give you my license, I'm going to give you the barrel of my gun." Simpson alleged that while she was still writing down the VIN number and was standing towards the front of the car on the driver's side, she saw Mrs. Sherrod go into the driver's seat area of the car, bend down under the driver's seat, and come out. Simpson stated that the two were again arguing and that Simpson was shocked that "this elderly woman had actually gone into her car and brought out a gun." Simpson told the deponent that she had said things like, "are you really going to get a gun over an accident" or "are you really going to pull a gun over a mirror" and that she was shocked that it had gotten to the point where Mrs. Sherrod had a gun in her hand. Simpson told the deponent that she began to leave immediately after Mrs. Sherrod retrieved the gun but then would stop herself and go back and confront Mrs. Sherrod because she was still upset and "couldn't believe this was happening." Simpson stated that Mrs. Sherrod then extended her arm and Simpson got into her car and left.

Deponent admitted that it seemed hard to believe that Simpson had continued to go

back and argue with Mrs. Sherrod even though Mrs. Sherrod had a gun in her hand but that it was not fair for him as a detective to simply disbelieve her statement without any confirmation that she was lying. Deponent testified that therefore he went to look for the videotape.

Questions that Detective McHugh asked D. Simpson About the Gun

Q. "Did you look at her hand?"

A. "No."

Q. "Up until the time you left, did you ever look at her hand?"

A. "I don't think I did. I don't know."

Deponent testified that after Simpson gave him a narrative of the event, he began to ask her more specific follow-up questions. Deponent asked Simpson what the gun looked like and Simpson responded that it was black, but she didn't know how to describe it because she "didn't know guns" and did not know the different makes and models of guns. Deponent then asked Simpson questions trying to help her to describe the gun. He explained that he asked her whether it was like a cowboy gun or like a gun that police would carry because it has been his experience that victims who don't know guns have seen enough TV to know the difference between a revolver with a cylinder in the middle and a modern gun with a clip. At this point, Simpson told the deponent that she has a family member who is a police officer and that that is the type of gun it was. Simpson told deponent that the gun was a semi-automatic "like my family member has."

Deponent was then questioned about Simpson's testimony during her deposition and was shown excerpts from the Simpson deposition. Deponent testified that he understood that Simpson testified that she did not see what was in Mrs. Sherrod's hand and confirmed that this was different from what Simpson initially told him. Deponent testified that the transcript to him indicated that Simpson did not look at what was in Mrs. Sherrod's hand but assumed there was something there because of the full context of the situation but noted that during the deponent's interview Simpson was "very clear about what happened [and] what she saw" and that Simpson's answers at that time were "strikingly different than what [deponent is] reading in [the] transcript." Deponent testified that when Simpson referred to a "collaboration" between herself and the deponent as to the description of the gun she may have been referring to the deponent asking her questions about revolvers versus police guns but other than that he was not aware of what she meant.

Deponent testified that right after he was assigned to the case, he reached out to Officer Patel and spoke to him on the phone. Officer Patel told deponent that his sergeant directed him to classify the incident as a threats report and not an assault with a dangerous weapon because of the delay in reporting. Deponent did not know whether the sergeant initially decided to categorize this as a threat or whether it was a lieutenant because he was not working that night. Deponent confirmed that when he initially got the case the charge was threats.

Deponent testified that he found it strange that Simpson waited seven hours before calling the police because he believed that this would be something that she would want to report sooner given the severity of the allegations. However, deponent testified that after Simpson explained the delay it made sense to him and he was no longer suspicious.

MCHUGH'S INVESTIGATION

Deponent testified that he was the lead investigator in this case and attended the witness conferences with the US Attorney's Office. Deponent testified that he has investigated armed robbery cases in the past where the gun was never recovered or where a fake gun was used, and this did not inhibit the investigation. Deponent confirmed that it was not essential to the prosecution of this case that he be told the make and model of the gun used but stated that it would be important that the gun be found because there would be a stronger case if the jury could be shown the gun. Deponent testified that he always tries to find all the evidence.

Deponent testified that after his interview with Simpson where she described the incident to the deponent, he knew who Mrs. Sherrod was and had traced her information based upon the information that Simpson gave to the deponent. Deponent knew Mrs. Sherrod's address and full name. Deponent testified that he did not apply for an arrest warrant at that time because he wanted to be thorough in his investigation, including obtaining the video footage, interviewing Mrs. Sherrod, and attempting to find and interview other witnesses. Deponent testified that there was no need right at that moment to rush something when he could take his time with the investigation and be thorough about it. Deponent testified that at that point he only had his interview with Simpson and the information in the police report as evidence but stated that this was "not enough" because although Mrs.

Sherrod fit the general description and was a registered owner of the vehicle, he would need either an admission from Mrs. Sherrod that she was at the scene of the accident or to do an "identification procedure."

Deponent testified that he visited Gingko Gardens on May 15 at 2:45 PM. Deponent explained that he wrote a narrative of the visit and that every time a detective takes a step in an investigation, they document this with a supplement in the electronic case file. Deponent testified that he took handwritten notes regarding who he spoke to at Gingko Gardens: [redacted].

Deponent testified that he obtained a video of the incident. He watched it on the computer in the flower shop then downloaded it and brought it back to the police station where he showed it to his supervisor, Lieutenant Richard Brady. Deponent also showed the tape to Sergeants Thomas Boone and David Edelstein. The video is not enhanced, and deponent confirmed that it is grainy and not clear. Deponent did not recall seeing a twentyish year-old Black man going in and out of Gingko Gardens in the video and never interviewed a man of this description. Deponent testified that he did not recall interviewing a man named ██████. Deponent testified that the video captured the incident from 11:10 a.m. to 11:27 a.m. but the deponent could not recall how much of the video he downloaded but remembers the incident being seventeen minutes long.

Deponent testified that after he viewed the videotape, he went to the Sherrods' home on May 16 at 12:45 p.m. Deponent could not recall whether he called Mrs. Sherrod before going to the house and did not remember whether her phone number was available to him at that time. Deponent knocked on the Sherrods' door but no one answered.

Deponent testified that he first contacted the Prince George's County Police Department about the investigation into Mrs. Sherrod on May 16th. Before deponent went to the home, on May 15 on 1:15PM, he placed information into WALES (Washington Area Law Enforcement System), a local database where police include lookouts for people, and NCIC (National Crime Information Center), a nation-wide database managed by the FBI where all missing persons, stolen vehicles, felony vehicles, and stolen property are listed.

Deponent testified that when he included "If the vehicle is located, hold all occupants and seize the vehicle as evidence," he believed that officers would stop the vehicle and not allow the occupant to leave or release the vehicle until the deponent or another officer could arrive at the scene. Deponent testified that he indicated the vehicle was involved in an assault with a dangerous weapon but did not believe that officers would necessarily use guns to stop the Sherrods' vehicle. Deponent testified that the "whole point" of putting a notice into NCIC or WALES is so that officers would use caution when approaching the vehicle or the occupants but claimed that he did not have an expectation that the officers who stopped them might use their guns as a way to effect the stop of the vehicle. Deponent admitted that he would not be surprised if an officer drew their gun when stopping the vehicle if they felt it was needed for their personal safety, but this was a "personal decision."

Deponent testified that he was aware that the Sherrods' vehicle was ultimately stopped and that the Sherrods may have been approached with guns out when the stop was made. Deponent testified that he knew because he had read the complaint.

Deponent testified that at the time these reports were entered he had not obtained a search or arrest warrant for Mrs. Sherrod but admitted that in these requests he asked law enforcement to hold Mrs. Sherrod. Deponent stated that he gave the main number for the MPD request, but that whoever was reached at the office could then contact him on his cell phone. Deponent stated that if he were unavailable when the vehicle was stopped any on-duty detective could get the case number from NCIC, access the reports, and go to the scene to handle the stop. Deponent further stated that at the time he entered the request into NCIC and WALES he had not shown Simpson the video and stated that he did not have a need to show her the video. Deponent testified that they would not typically do a photo array in this type of situation because the victim identified the person and gave their name, so they would only do a single confirmation photo.

Deponent testified that during his investigation he checked law enforcement databases, including PG County, Maryland Watch Center, and the ATF, to search whether Mrs. or Mr. Sherrod had a firearm registered to them. He did not find that either of them had such a firearm. Deponent stated that this did not impact the investigation because in Maryland you were not required to register a gun before a certain year, so it was possible that the Sherrods owned weapons that were not registered.

Deponent testified that even though the videotape was grainy and not of good quality, he believed that it corroborated Simpson's version of the story. Deponent admitted that at this point in the investigation the only evidence was Simpson's statement and the videotape.

Deponent testified that he did not believe Mrs. Sherrod's version of events. He did not tell her what Simpson had said beyond that she alleged that Mrs. Sherrod pulled a gun on her. Mrs. Sherrod told deponent that if she had anything in her hand it was a notebook and a pen. Deponent admitted that the video is not clear enough to see what Mrs. Sherrod had in her hand.

Deponent testified that he did not apply for an arrest warrant after his conversation with Mrs. Sherrod because he spoke to the prosecutors, Kacie Watson and Jennifer Kirkhoff and to his supervisor and everyone agreed that the deponent should first find and search the car and possibly search the Sherrods' home. Deponent testified that the two prosecutors watched the video with him and agreed that it showed Mrs. Sherrod pointing a gun at Simpson. Deponent testified that even though the video was not clear enough to see what is in

Mrs. Sherrod's hand, you could see her arm outstretched in front of her body and "to anyone in law enforcement, that's an indication of someone pointing a gun at somebody else." The video did not rule out that Mrs. Sherrod was holding a notebook, but deponent believed Simpson's version of events and that the video corroborated her story and so did the US Attorney's Office.

SEARCH WARRANT

Deponent testified he did not apply for a no-knock warrant to search the Sherrods' home, but he did assist and requested assistance with obtaining a regular search warrant for the home. Deponent stated that there was no reason for this to be a no-knock warrant, which is typical in drug cases or other cases where evidence could be easily destroyed. Deponent contacted Michael McAveety, a detective in PG County who worked in the district where the Sherrods' home was, to assist the deponent with obtaining the search warrant. Deponent knew McAveety because they were part of an interstate group of officers who share information regarding auto theft related crimes together. McAveety would contact the deponent to get copies of reports at different times, but this was the extent of their interaction.

After contacting McAveety, deponent sent McAveety a copy of an affidavit draft that deponent had prepared, which summarized his investigation up until that point. Deponent testified that McAveety did not work for the Bowie Police Department but that the PG County Police Department and the Bowie Police Department do work together. Detective Simmons was the affiant on the search warrant. Simmons, a City of Bowie detective, was assigned to a robbery unit in PG County and knew McAveety. McAveety gave Simmons the task of writing the warrant because Simmons "needed experience in writing warrants and going through the process." This warrant was written early in Simmons' career. Deponent testified that Simmons made changes from the draft warrant that deponent sent in, including copying the information provided onto a template, adding the items to be searched for and adding the affiant's background.

Deponent testified that neither Simmons nor McAveety viewed the videotape prior to making the application for the warrant. Deponent could not recall whether he ever showed the video to the detectives and testified that the videotape did not influence obtaining the warrant beyond what was contained in the deponent's summary of facts. Deponent confirmed that Simmons and McAveety relied solely on deponent's investigation in going forward with the search warrant application. Deponent testified that he remembered writing everything in the summary of events sent to Simmons and McAveety.

VEHICLE STOP

Deponent testified that a traffic stop was effected on the Sherrods' vehicle on June 24th,

2015. The vehicle passed a license plate reader a 1:17PM and would have been stopped moments later by Capitol Police. Deponent was not present when the stop was made. Someone from Capitol Police called the MPD office and deponent's lieutenant notified deponent that the vehicle was stopped by the Capitol. Deponent estimated that he arrived at the scene of the stop approximately ten minutes after the phone call was placed to the MPD office.

When deponent arrived at the scene of the stop, he saw the Mercedes on the side of the road with Mr. and Mrs. Sherrod sitting inside of the vehicle. Officers were standing outside. Deponent spoke to a Capitol police officer who told deponent that the officer knew that this was the vehicle the deponent was looking for but did not believe the people inside the vehicle were the suspects the deponent was looking for. Deponent notified the officer that these were, in fact, the people he was looking for and the officer expressed disbelief because of the Sherrods' age. Deponent told the officer that the Sherrods were the suspects in the case and that the offense was on video but did not tell the officer that you could not see what was in Mrs. Sherrod's hand in the video.

Deponent testified that he spoke to Mrs. Sherrod first. He observed Mr. Sherrod sitting in the front passenger seat and Mr. Sherrod appeared calm. Deponent testified that an officer had told him that guns were drawn during the traffic stop but deponent could not recall who gave him this information. Deponent testified that he may have said to Mrs. Sherrod, "do you remember talking to me?" but that Mrs. Sherrod would have no idea who he was because they had never met before. Deponent then told Mrs. Sherrod that the investigation was still open into the event they had discussed on the phone about a month prior and asked whether Mrs. Sherrod would be okay with the deponent searching the vehicle to see whether there was a firearm inside. Deponent testified that he did not tell Mrs. Sherrod that she could either consent or they would seize the vehicle. Deponent testified that he could have seized the vehicle on that day but did not because there was no need to, as Mrs. Sherrod allowed deponent to search the vehicle. Deponent stated that he only would have had the vehicle seized if he was not there since they were not looking for any forensic evidence. Since deponent was searching for a gun, once he found no gun in the vehicle there was no reason to seize the car.

Deponent testified that after Mrs. Sherrod signed the document, he searched the vehicle and did not find any gun or contraband. Deponent confirmed that at this point Mrs. Sherrod had denied having a gun, that there were no guns registered according to Maryland and the ATF, and no gun was found during a search of the vehicle.

Deponent testified that after the traffic stop, he asked Mrs. Sherrod to accompany him to the First District for questioning but she did not do so. Deponent did not arrest Mrs. Sherrod at that time. The conversation ended when Mrs. Sherrod refused to come in and give a recorded statement and told deponent that she would not speak to him anymore without an attorney. Deponent claimed that Mr. or Mrs. Sherrod could have walked away at any time after they were stopped but before the search ended but stated that he did not tell the Sherrods that they could leave or go home if they had wanted to. Deponent admitted that he had his service weapon with him at this time. Deponent stated that he did not know what he would have done if Mr. or Mrs. Sherrod had left during the search but maintained that the Sherrods were not under arrest at that time. Deponent then admitted that the Sherrods were not free to walk away during the search because the officers were investigating. Deponent estimated that the entire stop lasted less than thirty minutes.

INVESTIGATION AFTER THE VEHICLE STOP

Deponent asked Susan Wittrock, the ATF agent who ran the weapons checks for the deponent, to conduct a firearms registration check to see whether either of the Sherrods had purchased any weapons or had any weapons on file. The email was sent on June 24 at approximately 7:04 p.m. Deponent admitted that in this e-mail he told Wittrock that the video was not clear enough to see what is in Mrs. Sherrod's hand or for the U.S. Attorney's Office to sign a warrant. Deponent told Wittrock that Maryland had run a weapons check that did not turn up any registered guns and requested that she run a check to see if there were any purchase records prior to the 1990s. Deponent testified that he included the fact that the Sherrods were nearly eighty years old because he did not want Wittrock to think that he had typed the birth date incorrectly, as it was not common to deal with elderly suspects. Deponent admitted writing, "if it was not on video, not sure I would have believed it myself." Deponent stated that he did not have doubts about what happened but was shocked that three senior citizens had been in this situation, a situation that deponent characterized as "outrageous."

WARRANTS

Deponent testified that in the draft search warrant he wrote that he believed there was at that time probable cause to believe that there was evidence of illegal firearms in the Sherrods' home. Deponent testified that in his experience firearms are usually kept on a person, in their vehicle, or in their home. Deponent did not ask the officials in PG County to apply for a search warrant for the Sherrods' vehicle because the vehicle would likely have been stopped in DC, so this was unnecessary. Deponent stated that he believed this to be the case because he had numerous reads of the Sherrods' vehicle being in DC on a regular basis. Deponent testified that at the time he submitted the request for a search warrant for the Sherrods' home he had probable cause to arrest Mrs. Sherrod for the ADW. Deponent explained that he believed that the police department's position was that they had enough for probable cause for an arrest, but the U.S. Attorney's office has a different standard for which cases they will go forward with. Deponent testified that he was not familiar with the general order that required officers to go to the grand jury intake assistant at the U.S. Attorney's office and have them sign off on it in order to get an arrest warrant in DC. Deponent testified that for a case like this only the US Attorney's Office could authorize an arrest warrant. Deponent testified that he did not believe the US Attorney's office had a different standard for probable cause than MPD but did believe the US Attorney's office had a different standard for determining which cases they wished to go forward with and what evidence they would like before proceeding with a case.

SEARCH OF THE SHERRODS' HOME

Deponent testified that he assisted members of the PG County Police Department in the execution of the search warrant of the Sherrods' home on the evening of July 7, 2015. Deponent stated that it was still light outside when they got to the home. Deponent was accompanied by members of the District 3 robbery unit, PG County police officers, Detective Simmons, the affiant on the warrant from Bowie, a sergeant, Detective Sergeant David Edelstein, a sergeant from the deponent's office, and Lieutenant Mtorek, the lieutenant in charge of investigation in that district. Mtorek was the official on the scene. Deponent testified that he informed the members of the department that they were searching for a gun and the officers at the scene were armed. The officers pulled their weapons while entering the home.

Deponent testified that the officer parked their cars in the street in front of the home. The PG County officers were driving marked police vehicles and there were also a few unmarked cars. Deponent arrived with his sergeant in an unmarked car. Deponent observed the PG officers approach the front door of the home and a few officers went to the back of the home. The sergeant knocked on the door and said that they were the police with a search warrant several times. Deponent testified that he was able to see a light on and the TV on in an upstairs bedroom. Deponent testified that he saw Mr. Sherrod come to the window and look down to see who was outside. The officers again shouted, "Police, please come to the door. We have a search warrant," but got no response. Deponent testified that he was not aware that Mr. Sherrod was legally blind.

Deponent had briefed the PG County officers in advance about the case, what they were looking for, and what tactics should be used to execute the warrant. Deponent stated that despite his direction, the execution of the warrant was ultimately up to the PG County officers' supervisors. Deponent testified that PG County usually uses their SWAT team for every violent-crime-related warrant with body armor, helmets, and flash-bangs, but testified that he did not want them to do that in this case.

Deponent testified that once the door was knocked down, he saw a line of officers go into the house. The officers were armed. Currently, deponent was still standing back with his sergeant. The officers shouted "Police, show us your hands. Police, search warrant." After about two or three minutes the sergeant came back outside and told the deponent and his sergeant that the scene was secure and they could go inside. When deponent entered the house, the Sherrods were in the living room on the first floor to the left upon entering the home and were sitting on the couch. They were not handcuffed then. There were officers in the living room, but their guns were not drawn at that point. Deponent testified that the Sherrods were not free to leave.

Deponent testified that once he got inside, he and his sergeant talked to the Sherrods, showed them a copy of the search warrant, and identified themselves. Deponent told them that the officers were there looking for a firearm that was used in the commission of the offense that they had previously talked about and that their car had been searched about. Deponent told the Sherrods that they did not want to inconvenience them any longer than they already had but they would have to conduct a full search of the house. Deponent told the Sherrods that "it would be great" if they could tell him where the gun was and that the officers could then simply seize it and be on their way. The Sherrods both responded and said that they did not have a gun and there was not a gun in the house. Deponent testified that they completed a search of the home and did not find a gun.

Deponent testified that he participated in the search of the home by searching the upstairs bedroom with his sergeant, searching the kitchen area, and looking around in the basement. The other officers searched all the other rooms in the home. Deponent stated that they looked all over the home and that they were to look through drawers or other containers and remove the contents. They did not put them back when they were finished. Deponent agreed that when the officers left, the Sherrods' home was in disarray. Deponent stated that during the search Mrs. Sherrod appeared upset and angry. Deponent recalled Mr. Sherrod sitting there calmly. Deponent could not recall whether the door was damaged when it was broken down and did not know how the officers opened the door. Deponent assumed that the officers used a tool.

ARREST WARRANT

Deponent testified that after the search he applied for an arrest warrant for Mrs. Sherrod. He admitted that he did not have any additional evidence at that time than what he had when he e-mailed Ms. Wittrock and told her that there was not enough evidence for the US Attorney's Office to sign a warrant. Deponent stated that the intervening events since he took Simpson's statement had not made his case weaker but did not make it any better.

Deponent testified that at the time he applied for the arrest warrant he was the sole investigator. Deponent included that the video was not clear enough to see what was in Mrs. Sherrod's hand and that Ms. Sherrod denied ever producing a weapon. Deponent confirmed that this warrant was sworn to on July 10, 2015, three days after the search of the Sherrods' home found no gun.

MRS. SHERROD'S ARREST

Deponent testified that he was contacted by an attorney who claimed to represent Mrs. Sherrod and asked whether there was an active warrant for her arrest. Deponent responded that there was. A day or so later, deponent was contacted by a second attorney and asked the same question to which he responded that there was. Deponent testified that he believed that the first attorney was David Schertler. Deponent denied knowing Mr. Schertler but recalled speaking to him and telling him there was a warrant for Mrs. Sherrod's arrest. Deponent denied giving Mr. Schertler any facts of the case. Deponent stated that he ultimately dealt with Attorney Brian McDaniel. Deponent stated that he did not share any facts of the case with Mr.

McDaniel but only told him that an arrest warrant was issued, and that deponent was trying to arrange for the most convenient way to have Mrs. Sherrod turn herself in and to have Mr. McDaniel come with her.

Deponent testified that he and Mr. McDaniel arranged for Mrs. Sherrod to turn herself in at the First District on M Street SW. Deponent explained that when he arranged for people to turn themselves in, he advised them to arrive at around 5 a.m. so they could be processed, transported down to court, and arraigned on the same day. If the person were to come the night before they would be forced to spend the night in jail. The Sherrods came in at exactly 5 a.m. and were accompanied by Attorney McDaniel. Mrs. Sherrod was taken to an interview room with Attorney McDaniel and advised of her Miranda warnings. Mrs. Sherrod invoked her right not to answer any questions. Mrs. Sherrod asked to review the video and deponent set up his laptop and showed Mrs. Sherrod and Attorney McDaniel the video. Deponent asked Mrs. Sherrod whether she wanted to discuss anything after having seen the video and she said no. Deponent was not present for the entirety of when Mrs. Sherrod and Attorney McDaniel looked at the video but may have been there for part of it. Deponent testified that this entire interaction was recorded. During this time period, deponent did not ask Mrs. Sherrod or Attorney McDaniel anything about the events of the case.

After the parties viewed the videotape, deponent took Mrs. Sherrod to the cellblock at the First District where she was processed. Deponent then went back to his desk and completed the arrest paperwork. Mrs. Sherrod was then processed (fingerprinted and photographed) and taken down to court. Deponent was not aware whether Mrs. Sherrod was kept in a cell during this process but believed that she was. Deponent also believed that Mrs. Sherrod was handcuffed during this time but was not shackled. Deponent stated that after he gave Mrs. Sherrod to processing, he did not see her for the rest of the day. Deponent was told that Mrs. Sherrod was transported to the central cellblock at 300 Indiana Avenue NW. Deponent stated that this was the same cellblock where all of the previous people from the night before would be held regardless of the crime that they were charged with. Deponent testified that he was told that Mrs. Sherrod had a need to eat and take medication at set intervals and deponent alerted the cellblock technician to make sure this was taken care of. Deponent testified that Mrs. Sherrod was released from arraignment court on personal recognizance and given a preliminary hearing date on the same day.

PRELIMINARY HEARING

Deponent testified that he next spoke to Simpson at the first witness conference for the grand jury. Deponent believed that Ms. Walters had reached out to Simpson to inform her that she needed to come in for the grand jury hearing.

Deponent testified that a preliminary hearing took place in DC Superior Court, Courtroom 301. Deponent was called as a witness for the government. Deponent stated that he had never seen a copy of the transcript from his testimony at this hearing. Deponent stated that the magistrate found probable cause because of deponent's testimony. Deponent could not recall his testimony.

MEETINGS WITH THE U.S. ATTORNEY'S OFFICE

Deponent testified that he could not recall the first time that he went to the U.S. Attorney's Office for meetings regarding the case but confirmed these meetings occurred. Deponent first met with Ms. Walters and Simpson was present at this meeting. Deponent stated that from the best of his recollection the first meeting was Ms. Walters' first interview with Simpson and Ms. Walters was preparing Simpson to go before the grand jury. Ms. Walters walked Simpson through the events and asked some personal questions about Simpson. Deponent testified that at this meeting there were some inconsistencies in Simpson's recollection of the events. Deponent stated this was the first time he learned that Simpson had some memory issues and other nonspecific mental health issues. Due to Simpson's inconsistencies, the prosecutor decided not to put Simpson in front of the grand jury on that date. Deponent stated that Simpson was agitated, emotional, dramatic, and animated during this first meeting. Deponent stated that Simpson's demeanor was "completely different" from the first time he had met her. Deponent stated most of the inconsistencies in Simpson's story was about the gun, which she now described as a silver revolver as opposed to a black semi-automatic handgun. Deponent stated that despite this inconsistency, it was not his place to stop the prosecution at that point in the process.

Deponent stated that when Simpson finished the interview and left, deponent discussed the interview with Ms. Walters. Deponent stated that Simpson's mental health issues concerned him, as well as the inconsistencies in her story and her change in demeanor. Deponent stated that when they had explored the description of the gun with Simpson in more detail, she backed off of the idea that it was silver and stated that she "got a glint of the metal" that was pointed at her. Deponent stated that the other parts of Simpson's story was consistent. Deponent stated that he still believed Simpson and believed that Ms. Walters did also. Ultimately, it was decided to bring Simpson back a second time within a week or so. Deponent stated that Simpson's behavior was consistent with someone who went "off their meds." Deponent stated Simpson was still maintaining that Mrs. Sherrod "put a gun in her face" but deponent stated this characterization was his own words and Simpson simply said that Mrs. Sherrod pointed a gun at her. Deponent testified that Simpson told him that she had memory issues and trouble remembering things. Deponent testified that there was nothing that stopped him from speaking to Simpson between the time of the first interview and the date of the first meeting with the US Attorney.

Deponent testified that Simpson returned about a week later and they had a similar conversation. Deponent did not speak to Simpson between these two meetings, although there was nothing that would have stopped him from doing so. Deponent did not show Simpson the tape during this time period. Simpson did make comments that she would be able to more fully answer the questions that were posed to her if she were able to see the tape, but Simpson never directly asked to see the tape. Deponent testified that he had discussed whether to show the tape to Simpson with the prosecutors, but they had ultimately decided against it because they did not want to color Simpson's testimony. Deponent indicated that if they were to show Simpson the tape, they would need to reveal this fact to the grand jury. Deponent testified that he had no reason to doubt the veracity of Simpson's narrative during the investigation and that the investigation would not have changed had he been aware of her mental health issues. During the second meeting, the parties again went through the series of events and Simpson was asked questions. At this meeting, Simpson's demeanor was more in line with what it was the first time the deponent interviewed her and was mostly consistent with her story until they reached the part about the gun. During this interview, she simply stated that she got a glint of a metal object in Mrs. Sherrod's hand while hearing Mr. Sherrod say, "Get the gun, get the gun." Deponent stated that he believed Mrs. Sherrod had a gun because the two women had been arguing for quite some time, but after Mrs. Sherrod went back to her car Ms. Simpson left fairly quickly. The deponent indicated that something must have happened to make Simpson leave.

Deponent testified that he believed Simpson went in front of the grand jury on the way to her second meeting. After that meeting, deponent did not meet with Ms. Walters and Ms. Simpson about the case but did testify in front of the grand jury himself. Deponent testified that he did include Simpson's inconsistencies during the preparation sessions in his grand jury testimony. Deponent stated that he did not talk to Simpson after the grand jury and that the grand jury voted not to indict. Deponent testified that Ms. Walters notified Simpson that the grand jury did not indict.

SIMPSON LETTER AND CONTACT WITH MCHUGH

Deponent testified that he had not seen the letter Simpson wrote to the US District Judge who was presiding over this case. Deponent testified that he did tell Simpson that Mrs. Sherrod was not indicted, but this occurred "months later" after Ms. Walters had already notified her. Deponent testified that Simpson called him on the date that she was served with the papers in this case and asked whether he had information. Deponent told Simpson that he was also being sued and that he could not offer her any advice about what to do. Deponent advised Simpson to consult with an attorney. During that conversation, Simpson asked deponent whether it was true that Mrs. Sherrod was not indicted, and deponent confirmed this was true. Deponent stated that other than that conversation, he had not spoken to Simpson since the grand jury.

CHAPTER 20

The Decision

On September 25, 2018, Judge Rudolph Contreras ruled on the Motion for Summary Judgment of the United States District Court of the District of Columbia, D. Simpson and Detective McHugh. After hundreds of legal documents including discovery depositions, briefs, filings, exhibits, and many conferences and meetings, the judge's final order was signed. The settlement conference involved three groups of attorneys and insurance companies on behalf of the plaintiffs and defendants to negotiate damages. There were starts, cancellations, restarts, and then finally a round-robin of monetary lobs back and forth. This was the judicial system in action.

We sat in a freezing cold room for several days in negotiations. The room was so cold our eyes turned blood red and we all had to put on coats. There were cockroaches in the bathroom as we sat watching attorneys move from room to room with legal pads. Sitting there for hours, after a two-year long fight for justice and potentially going to trial, we learned about the politics of settlements. This was when everyone showed their true hearts and interests. Attorney Bynum said, "If everyone leaves the room mad, then it is a good settlement."

I did not know what he meant but I came to learn. We did not know that the attorneys that represented us, and now were in our hearts like family, would become what we have heard about attorneys concerning trust. That their interests would overcome our own. That two years of fellowship, prayer, and gatherings in our home breaking bread would now evolve into them needing to protect their future interests. That they would look us in our eyes and break our hearts making statements such as, "We are not going to trial," "We have invested a lot of money in this case," "We are tired and exhausted," and the final killer that was like a dagger in our hearts, "Detective McHugh would lose his job if the constitutional claims..."

My mind was in shock. I almost lost control of my bladder when the words, "Detective McHugh would lose his job if..." How cold, callous, and painful, but it all came down to needing to keep their status with the District of Columbia government who were much bigger than us. Their future depended on meeting somewhere in the middle with the Attorney General's Office so their relationship would remain intact for potential referrals in the future. As entrepreneurs and business owners, we understood. But the last indignation was to know that after all our pain, humiliation, degradation, fear and suffering, our attorneys did not even say goodbye to us as we walked down the hall and went our separate ways that Friday at 5 p.m. There was no, "Keep in touch," "Thank you for being great clients" (other than giving information when they needed it), or "We are sorry Detective McHugh wasn't fired" for his misconduct and unscrupulous abuse of power over two senior citizens.

Moreover, the initial seed of self-centeredness and self-interest was laid by our attorneys. Gene and I were set up to fail from the beginning by our lawyers, although we did not know it at the time.

We celebrated at the Ballantyne Hotel in Charlotte, North Carolina when we read the complaint filed to launch our lawsuit. We rejoiced and lifted praise of thanksgiving that justice would come to us. We were in awe of how many counts there were on our behalf that elucidated the 'crimes' against us by a police officer, a private citizen, and the government. And we stopped breathing for a few seconds when we turned to the last page and saw $10,000,000 not once but twice. The lawsuit sought damages in the amount of $20,000,000.00. Yes, that is right $20,000,000.00. We jumped for joy into the early morning. It felt like justice was around the corner, but that was only the monetary part of punishing those who hurt law abiding citizens for their own personal motivations. What we did not know is that the financial damage calculation is based on as we were told, "the value of the case." Well, if the value of the case is a realistic calculation, then we were owed quite a bit more money.

For those who end up in our predicament, let me tell you what "the value of the case" really means. It means that your lawyers can use that money to go to their bank to get a business loan based on cases in their portfolio. It means the case is their insurance policy to use to obtain lines of credit from banks to keep their business running. It means the value of the case from our perspective was never a consideration.

Although lawyers who make 'contingency fee agreements' with clients are a blessing, clients need to ensure that the energy and devotion to the case is respected. Our attorneys lived up to that ideal even though in the end, the expenses that we were charged for the case were more than we expected. But that is the business of legal representation. The unknown is the resulting return on their investment, and starting out with a demand that does not immediately put the defendant or opponents in a defensive posture gives more opportunity for an amenable settlement, time and cost savings, undue stress and character assaults to the innocent, and enables the pursuit of justice in a more fair and equitable manner. But, that line of credit!

Victory also meant that lawyers used our case as a marketing tool to promote their capabilities and services including using our story produced by a local television station on their websites. We are at peace with the outcome of our relationship with our attorneys. We wish them well and feel God put them in our lives when we needed them most. But lessons learned.

Thankfully, we were also blessed with a great judge. He immediately saw the injustice in our case by issuing an exhaustive Memorandum of Opinion in February 2017. He stated:

This case involves allegations that, if true, drastically undermine the integrity of a District of

Columbia police officer and illustrate the damage that the unscrupulous use of power can inflict upon citizens of the state. Detective Phillip McHugh allegedly discovered that the other driver's report was false, yet relentlessly used the criminal justice system to harass the Sherrods.

It took almost two years to get to Judge Contreras' final decision concerning the Motion for Summary Judgment of the Defendants. We were told it could be longer, but our attorneys pushed for a fast process because of our age and health status. Obviously, it was in everyone's best interest because if we died or became seriously ill, they would have lost their investment.

Judge Contreras' decision can be summed up simply as the judge denied all the claims of Detective McHugh and the District Columbia except those related to the actions of the Capitol Hill police officers and the Prince George's County police officers, because they proceeded to act based on the false information provided in the warrant by Detective

McHugh. He also **denied** all the claims of the Defendant, D. Simpson.

From the lessons we gleaned from our experience, we want to help those who may find themselves in a battle like the one we endured. First, sadly, many Americans do not have any savings to obtain good legal representation in the event they find themselves being falsely accused of a crime. The police know this, and that is why many unscrupulous officers use their power to cause pain to citizens. They have goals. They want to get promotions. This does not help either. Some officers are on a mission to 'clean up society' and use their power to do so. Sadly, implicit bias or unconscious bias plays a role in the process. Stereotypical thinking based on gender, race, skin color, weight and other factors impact decision making even if it is unconsciously done. While this is a neat way of saying it, it is basically the seed that produces the offspring called 'racism.'

Racism is the use of human traits and capacities that use racial differences resulting in inherent superiority of a particular race. A police officer who had as much information as Detective McHugh had about D. Simpson who continued to believe her throughout his investigation is a dangerous police officer to citizens. Conversely, D. Simpson was a stereotypical example of how racists view African Americans. She was wrong. She hit our car. She was driving without valid insurance, but we put a gun in her face. Two senior citizens driving a Mercedes Benz, husband and wife, going to buy flowers. She did have mental health issues, but she was validated by Detective McHugh because of his implicit bias. But that needs to be obvious to the legal representation you seek. Our attorneys did not want to go that route. They did not want to go public or to the press. I am sure they had a good reason for that, but it may not have been the best strategy.

Secondly, we want to share tips for getting good legal representation. The most important tip is to interview the attorney. Do not fall into the trap of them interviewing you! We did not have a lot of time to find a lawyer for our civil case, so we felt blessed to obtain counsel at the midnight hour. Your attorney will interview you as well; be sure to be honest. Here are some questions you might ask when interviewing an attorney for representation:

- What experience do you have in the type of legal matter that is needed?
- How long have you been in practice?
- What is your track record of success?
- What are your fees and how are they structured?
- Do you carry malpractice insurance? If so, how much?
- Who else will be working on my case and what are their rates?
- Do you outsource any key legal tasks?
- What additional costs may be involved?
- How often will I be billed?

- Can you provide references from other clients?
- Do you have a written fee agreement or representation agreement?
- How will you inform me of developments in my case?
- How often will you update me on the status of my case, and how responsive will you be to my calls, emails and inquiries concerning the case?

After you determine how comfortable you are with the retainer or legal agreement, understand that attorney-client relationship is personal and requires trust on both sides and commitment to truth and justice. Careful planning and forethought along the way improves the relationship and the outcome of the case for both parties.

CONCLUSION

NEW BEGINNINGS

I felt like I could breathe again. I looked younger, felt younger, and was thinking younger. We were finally free, but I was not fooled. The experience was not totally out of my spirit. It was merely that all the legal work related to filing a civil lawsuit against the District of Columbia, Metropolitan Police Department, and a private citizen, D. Simpson was over. The emotional and physical toll still weighed on our shoulders hidden beneath the smiles we both wore.

Four years have passed since 2015. During that time, we missed many fun days filled with joy, smiles, and laughter. We lost friends whose funerals we did not attend because we simply did not have the energy or mental stamina to go forward with any more stress or sadness. Now, we were moving forward with the goal of reviving our spirits, our life, our souls with a renewed sense of hope that better days were ahead. We had passed through the storm and were looking to once again celebrate that God had given us another day. Thankfully, other than the impact of stress that was unforeseen in our inward parts, we were still healthy.

No one but God knew the long-range impact. There was no amount of money that could repay us for the time we lost because of this injustice. Now, we sought to help others: to give advice, to be a role model to those who may sadly experience the power of the justice system wielded without thought or care against ordinary citizens. It was our turn, and we were going to seize the day and tell the world our story.

"Hi, Gene, this is Nathan."

"Hey, man, how are you doing?"

Nathan Parker is a dear friend of ours whom we have known for over forty years. We met as entrepreneurs at various events and conferences for business owners. Nathan specializes in marketing, promotions, and communications.

A year ago, we had shared with him that we filed a civil suit against the District of Columbia, Metropolitan Police Department, and a private citizen. Nathan begged us to go to the media to share our story, but that was not part of the strategy. Nathan regularly checked in with us on the status of the case and whether we were ready to tell our story.

"Gene, are you and Vash ready?" he asked.

"Yes, I think we are," replied Gene. "Let me talk to Vash."

In minutes, we let Nathan know we were ready and asked when he could meet with us. Nathan is eager and was outside of our door two days later. Looking out the window, I saw Nathan walking up the driveway. He had on a business casual outfit, beige with an over vest, and a bow tie, which he was known for. His brown leather briefcase, stuffed with papers, matched his buttercream complexion. He was ready for business, albeit with close friends.

I opened the door, and immediately he gave

me a big hug. Nathan is a warm and friendly person. The last time we saw each other, we were sailing on his sailboat on the Chesapeake Bay. Being the savvy businessperson that he is, Nathan owns and operates a sailboat company for cruises, fishing, special events, and relaxing on the bay.

"Hey, Vash, it is great to see you."

"You too, Nathan. Really good to see you. Thanks for coming."

Gene made his way to the door. "Hey, Nathan," he said as they locked in a bear hug that seemed to last five minutes, including back slapping. "Come on in and sit down."

I decided to let them bond as men. Gene needed that, to sit and talk to an old male friend. They talked for about an hour before I came back into the room.

"Vash, I can't believe what happened to you all. You look the same though, just as pretty as you always have looked.

I smiled. "Thanks, Nathan, I don't feel like it. I feel old and battered, but better now."

"I bet," he said. "Now that this is all over, did you all get what you wanted?"

I didn't know how to answer that question and decided to skip it. Equating getting justice with money is a hard thing to do. Freedom doesn't have a price. Being accused of such a horrible crime and more importantly going to jail, has no price.

Nathan became our blessing. His expertise in media and his contacts in journalism would allow us to heal. We discussed strategies to get our story out to the public, so the citizens of the District of Columbia could learn about how a simple car accident could become the nightmare of their life. How their tax dollars were being used to bail out criminal and unconstitutional activities of their law enforcement members in particular a rogue police officer who used his authority without a conscience. Through this strategy, if implemented, Gene and I would start to get our power back. To find our own voice at a time where we were just coming up from air. Living in secret and not being able to talk about this ordeal had added to my post-traumatic stress disorder. His proposal was to tell our story on television, specifically the news.

Nathan reached out to WUSA, WJLA, CNN, NBC, and CBS news channels. He disseminated a wire through the channels he uses to get their attention. Then he called a well-known investigative reporter at WUSA9, Eric Flack. Two days later, Eric was sitting in our family room, along with his crew interviewing us about our experience. We were excited to tell our story, for the first time, in our own home from our perspective. We were seated on the sofa, and Gene began to cry as he retold the story and reflected on his pain of not being able to protect me.

In April 2019, I opened my eyes at 7 a.m. one morning to the sound of my voice and face on television. "Gene, Gene, oh my goodness that's me!" We couldn't believe it. There were thirty second teasers throughout the day, and that evening, WUSA9 featured our story for ten minutes on the news. The production of the story was professional, each clip they aired to promote the story was just right. Promotional clips were available on WUSA9's website, Facebook, YouTube, Twitter, Instagram, and other social media outlets. Eric gave the clips catchy names such as "Grandma, why are you in here?"

On a beautiful spring Sunday, just after Easter, Gene and I walked up the front steps of our church in Alexandria, Virginia, holding hands. We had been asked to speak before the congregation, now that our legal journey had come to an end. Our church had nearly 10,000 members and was regularly active in the community providing support and care to those in need spiritually, financially, and physically.

I had been impacted directly by the Jail Ministry whose lay leader, the Reverend Edward James, helped us greatly. Gene and I sat with the Reverend James on the first row of the church along with the church ministers and the diaconate.

Service started and I was ready to address the congregation. Upon hearing our names, both Gene and I stood to approach the pulpit, and into my hearing was thunderous applause from the congregation. Everyone knew about what happened to us, and all that we had been through. Looking out at our church family I could feel my heart racing, but it was from joy not fear, love not resentment, and peace not strife.

Gene stood by my side as I spoke into the microphone. "Good morning, church! Praise the Lord! We are back!" *Applause. Applause.* "As we reconnect back with you, our church family, we realize that the key to healing and moving forward with new beginnings is to forgive. The Bible says "forgiveness is the act of pardoning an offender. The Greek word "forgiveness" literally means to "let go." In Luke 11:4, it reads, "Forgive us our sins, for we ourselves also forgive everyone who is in debt to us." In order to heal we must let go of the resentment and give up any claim to be compensated for the hurt or loss we have suffered.

"They will never know how much they hurt us with the unscrupulous use of power they wielded upon us, but God knows. And He has taught us that we must forgive D. Simpson, Detective Philip McHugh, Chief of Police Cathy Lanier and Peter Newsham, Attorney David Jackson, D.C. Attorney General Karl Racine, and Mayor Muriel Bowser of the District of Columbia. To release the pain and assist with invoking forgiveness, I call up to God the names of those who inflicted unfair, unjust, and just plain wrong acts against me, my husband and my family. I pray that they or anyone in their family line never experience what we experienced. The act of forgiveness helps ease the post-traumatic stress disorder that I now live with in the recesses of my mind.

"I am blessed to tell my story. Healing involves telling the truth and being able to release the experience into the atmosphere and hearing of others by the spoken word. The spoken word takes flight and lands in the ears and experiences of others to use as they wish to survive this journey called life. It gives me great happiness to talk to others about my experience and to share the steps necessary to survive police misconduct, wrongdoing, and abuse of power.

"I am grateful that Gene and I were not killed or injured by the many interactions we experienced with the police and D. Simpson on Capitol Hill and at our own home. Many victims are killed or injured and never get to live to tell their stories. I pray for the families of those individuals, and now when I hear on the news that another young life has been taken by police brutality, I am pained knowing that could have been us. Two senior citizens just living our lives, innocently going about our day buying flowers without knowing what lurked ahead of us. In the course of a simple day, our journey was intersected by a mentally ill woman, a police officer whose ambition to clock in arrests and gun-charges without regard to the constitutional rights of citizens he vowed to protect, and the District government that failed us by unleashing its power without care and protecting their own interest at the expense of our lives. And, as our fourth President of the United States, Founding

Father and "Father of the "Constitution" and "Bill of Rights" wrote, "the essence of government is power, and power, lodged as it must be in human hands, will ever be liable to abuse."

"But God will have the final say. Let's push forward to help the innocent, especially mothers who find themselves in jail. Pray for those without resources to fight for their rights and to get justice for themselves. We will work with our last breath to help the poor seek justice in a system that swallows them up without regard to their constitutional rights. Church family, let us commit to social justice and change in this country. The fight for civil rights has not been won."

As Gene and I returned to our seat, along with Pastor James, we felt restored. I could feel the love, the standing ovation, the 'amens', the 'praise the Lord', coming from our church family. The organ began to play, and I woke up from this beautiful dream! Now, we continue to move forward and tell our story to all who will hear and read it.

About the Author

Vashti Sherrod was born in Filbert, South Carolina and later resided in Washington, DC. She graduated from Minor's Teacher's College and attended Cortez Peters School of Business-diploma for career opportunities in the federal government. To pursue her passion for Interior Design, she studied at Montgomery College in Silver Spring, Maryland. She is currently married and lives in Mitchellville, Maryland.

CPSIA information can be obtained
at www.ICGtesting.com
Printed in the USA
LVHW052025210221
679514LV00001B/90